The Secret
of the Miracle Economy

D1300061

The Secret
of the Miracle Economy:
different national attitudes
to competitiveness
and money

by
Richard Lynn

"The Secret of the Miracle Economy"

written in collaboration with

Ahmed Abdel-Khalek
Alexandria University, Egypt

Leandro Silva Almeida
Minho University, Portugal

Ruben Ardila
National University of Colombia, Bogota, Colombia

Adriana Baban
Institute of Hygiene & Public Health, Cluj-Napoca, Romania

Kyuhan Bae
Kookmin University, Seoul, Korea

Jimmy Chan
University of Hong Kong

Chong-Jen Chuang
National Taiwan University, Taiwan

Dafina Dalbokova
Medical Academy, Sofia, Bulgaria

Caroline Davis
York University, Canada

Danilo Donolo
University of Rio Cuarto, Argentina

Odile Dosnon
Institut National d'Etudes du Travail et d'orientation Professionelle, Paris, France

Bo Ekehammar
University of Stockholm, Sweden

Francois Gendre
University of Lausanne, Switzerland

Barbara Glenn
University College, Dublin, Ireland

Amer Hosin
Al Mustasiriyah University, Baghdad, Iraq

Sushil Jindal
Kurukshetra University, India

Cigdem Kagitcibasi
Bogazici University, Istanbul, Turkey

Rumina Kakati
Abu-Dhabi, United Arab Emirates

A Khaleque
University of Dhaka, Bangladesh

Chrysa Kiountouzis
Athens, Greece

Bruce Kirkcaldy
Dusseldorf, West Germany

David Lester
Richard Stockton College, Pomono, New Jersey, USA

Leon Lojk
Kranj, Yugoslavia

Juan Manso-Pinto
Conception University, Chile

José Martinez Selva
University of Murcia, Spain

Alicja Maurer
Krakow University, Poland

Tuntufye S Mwamwenda
University of Transkei, South Africa

George Meuris
Catholic University of Leuvain, Belgium

Ahmad Mirjafari
Shiraz University, Iran

Jitendra Mohan
Punjab University, India

Marcia Noce Nanci
Sao Paulo, Brazil

Chris Nunns
University of the Witwatersrand, Johannesburg, South Africa

M Pitariu
University of Cluj-Napoca, Romania

Yeshayahu Rim
Institute of Technology, Haifa, Israel

David Robinson
University of Sydney, Australia

Petra Rose
Amman, Syria

José Miguel Salazar
Central University of Venezuela, Caracas, Venezuela

Ralph Scott
University of Northern Iowa, Iowa, USA

Ming Singer
University of Canterbury, New Zealand

Pedro Solis-Camara
Division Biologia del Desarrollo, Guadalajura, Mexico

Sven Svebak
University of Bergen, Norway

Joshiharu Tachibana
Gifu University, Japan

Esther Tan
Institute of Education, Singapore

Claude Tapia
University of Tours, France

Bengü Balkir
Bogazici University, Istanbul, Turkey

Hirotsugu Yamauchi
Doshisha University, Kyoto, Japan

Bistra Zenova
Medical Academy, Sofia, Bulgaria

Li-zhang Zhuang
Beijing University of Posts and Telecommunications, China

British Library Cataloguing in Publication Data
Lynn, Richard, *1930 –*
    The secret of the miracle economy : different national
    attitudes to competitiveness and money.
    1. Economic conditions. Role of business enterprise.
    history
    I. Title   II. Social Affairs unit
    338.609

    ISBN 0-907631-41-X

The opinions expressed in The Secret of the Miracle Economy
*are those of the author, not of the Social Affairs Unit,
its Trustees, Advisors or Director.*

Book production by Crowley Esmonde Ltd
Typeset in Times by Harrison Typesetting, Whitton, Middlesex
Printed and bound in Great Britain by SRP Ltd., Exeter

Contents

		Page
	List of Tables	8
	Preface	11
1	Introduction: An Overview of the Study	13
2	Psychological Factors in Economic Growth	22
3	Design of the Study	43
4	The Work Ethic	48
5	Achievement Motivation	54
6	Mastery	57
7	Competitiveness	60
8	Achievement via Conformity	64
9	Valuation of Money	67
10	Attitudes to Saving	71
11	Occupational Preferences	74
12	Multiple Regression Analyses of the Contribution of Work Attitudes to Economic Growth	85
13	Factor Analysis of Work Attitudes Across Countries	91
14	Factor Analyses of Work Attitudes Within Countries	95
15	Epilogue	103
	Notes and References	109

List of Tables

		Page
1	Annual percentage rates of growth of output (GDP) in 12 countries at constant prices	22
2	Phases of productivity growth (GDP per man hour) 1870-1976	23
3	Rates of economic growth 1970-85 in the countries studied and per capita incomes in 1985	47
4	Mean scores of males and females on the Spence-Helmreich Work Ethic Scale	49
5	Means and standard deviations for the Spence-Helmreich Work Ethic Scale	50
6	Correlations between the Spence-Helmreich Work Ethic Scale, economic growth rates and per capita incomes	52
7	Means and standard deviations for the Ray-Lynn Achievement Motivation Scale	55
8	Correlations between the Ray-Lynn Achievement Motivation Scale, economic growth rates and per capita incomes	56
9	Means and standard deviations for the Spence-Helmreich Mastery Scale	58
10	Correlations between the Spence-Helmreich Mastery Scale, economic growth rates and per capita incomes	59
11	Means and standard deviations for the Spence-Helmreich Competitiveness Scale	61
12	Correlations between national means for Competitiveness and economic growth and per capita incomes	62

		Page
13	Means and standard deviations for the Gough Achievement via Conformity Scale	65
14	Correlations between the Gough Achievement via Conformity Scale, economic growth rates and per capita incomes	66
15	Means and standard deviations for the Valuation of Money Scale	68
16	Correlations between the Valuation of Money Scale, economic growth rates and per capita incomes	69
17	Means and standard deviations for the Attitudes to Savings Scale	72
18	Correlations between the Attitudes to Savings Scale, economic growth rates and per capita incomes	73
19	Means and standard deviations for evaluations of the occupation of doctor	75
20	Means and standard deviations for evaluations of the occupation of social worker	76
21	Means and standard deviations for evaluations of the occupation of company director	77
22	Means and standard deviations for the evaluations of the occupation of teacher	78
23	Means and standard deviations for the evaluations of the occupation of country landowner and farmer	79
24	Means and standard deviations for evaluations of the occupation of small business owner	80
25	Correlations between occupational preferences and economic growth rates and per capita incomes	83
26	Matrix of correlations derived from the 41 nation sample	86
27	Multiple regression analyses for psychological measures on rates of economic growth	87

		Page
28	Factor analysis of work attitudes across nations	92
29	Correlations between nations' factor scores on psychological measures and rates of economic growth	93
30	Correlations between nations' factor scores on psychological measures and per capita incomes	94
31	Varimax analysis of work attitudes in the United States	96
32	Varimax analysis of work attitudes in the United Kingdom	97
33	Varimax analysis of work attitudes in Australia	97
34	Varimax analysis of work attitudes in New Zealand	98
35	Varimax analysis of work attitudes in Singapore	99
36	Varimax analysis of work attitudes in Hong Kong	100
37	Varimax analysis of work attitudes in China	100
38	Varimax analysis of work attitudes in Japan	101

Preface

For the best part of a century theories have been advanced on the part played by psychological attitudes and values in economic growth and the complementary effects of economically determined standards of living on psychological attitudes and values. The most straightforward way of testing these theories is by the measurement of psychological attitudes and values in the populations of a large number of countries and examining whether the theoretical relationships with economic growth rates and incomes are present.

To collect data of this kind is a fairly difficult task which necessarily involves collaboration between a large number of individuals working in many different countries. Indeed, hitherto the task has apparently proved too daunting to be undertaken and it is believed that this is the first attempt to collect extensive data which would bear on the question of the relationship of psychological attitudes and values to economic growth and incomes. As an initial study of new ground, the work will no doubt be found to have weaknesses. It is to be hoped that others will be encouraged to develop further this approach to the measurement of psychological attitudes and values in a number of different countries and will be able to benefit from any weaknesses which may appear in this initial study.

I should like to record my appreciation of the help I have received from a number of sources in carrying out the study. These include the collaborators in the 43 countries from which the data were collected; the Trustees of the Esmée Fairbairn Foundation who awarded a grant for carrying out the research; Dr Digby Anderson, Director of the Social Affairs Unit in London, for his encouragement and advice; Susan Hampson, who worked as research assistant on the project and carried out a number of statistical computations; and to Mrs Betty Hemphill for her secretarial assistance.

Richard Lynn
University of Ulster
COLERAINE
Northern Ireland

1 Introduction: An overview of the study

This book presents the results of a study of attitudes to work among university students in 43 countries. The reason for undertaking the study was to determine whether national differences in work attitudes bear any relationship to rates of economic growth and per capita incomes. Several theories have been proposed that such relationships exist but they have never been satisfactorily tested and the testing of these theories is the principal objective of the study. This opening chapter presents a general overview of the results and conclusions, leaving details of the theories and findings to be presented in the subsequent chapters.

1.   Work attitudes and economic growth

Theories of the role played by psychological factors in economic growth go back to the early years of the century when Max Weber advanced the thesis of the Protestant work ethic as a major factor in the development of capitalism.[1]

Weber noted that in the later middle ages the most economically advanced European societies were Venice and the other city states of Northern Italy, Spain, Portugal and France. At this time the Northern European countries of Germany, the Low Countries, Scandinavia and England were economic backwaters. But in the sixteenth century the Reformation swept away the Roman Catholic Church in the northern countries and replaced it with the Protestant religions. From this time onwards the countries of Northern Europe began to prosper economically and draw ahead of those in southern Europe and it was Protestant England which led the field in the agricultural and industrial revolutions.

Weber thought that the association between Protestantism and economic growth was no accident. He proposed that the association arose because the Protestant religions stressed individuals' personal responsibility for their own lives, approved of wordly achievement and in some cases held that success in the world was a sign of grace. By contrast, Roman Catholicism placed greater value on poverty and withdrawal from the world in the monastery. It was the value system of Protestantism, Weber argued, that encouraged the peoples of northern Europe to work for worldly success and grow affluent in the process.

In contemporary times the concept of the work ethic has been shorn of its Protestant association and applied more widely to the problem of national differences in rates of economic growth. In the post World War Two period one of the most striking phenomena has been the rapid economic growth rates in the five East Asian countries, Japan, South Korea, Taiwan, Hong Kong and Singapore. Woronoff gives a good account of these in his book *Asia's Miracle Economies*[2] and Harvard economist David Landes discussed the question at the 1989 annual conference of the American Economics Association in a lecture with the arresting title of *Why are we so rich and they so poor?*[3] The upshot of these accounts is that economists really have no idea why the East Asian economies have made such spectacular economic progress and are forced to speculate about the presence of psychological forces such as a strong work ethic in the population.

Weber's theory of the work ethic was the first of several theories of economic growth which emphasised the significance of people's attitudes to work. Three later theories are particularly important. In the 1930s Joseph Schumpeter stressed the importance of the individual entrepreneur as the prime mover in economic growth, and he speculated about the psychology of the entrepreneur. He suggested that strong feelings of competitiveness are probably the principal motivation for entrepreneurs, consisting principally in the drive to prove themselves better than other people.

The next important theory appeared in 1961 with the publication of David McClelland's book *The Achieving Society*.[4] McClelland advanced the concept of what he called 'achievement motivation' consisting of a motive to do a job well and achieve a standard of excellence. He measured the strength of this commitment to excellence by an examination of the literature of a number of societies. He argued that the strength of achievement motivation in the population was a major factor responsible for economic growth and he traced out this relationship in a number of societies such as England from the sixteenth to the twentieth centuries and the United States over the last century or so.

The fourth major contribution to this question has been Wiener whose book *English Culture and the Decline of the Industrial Spirit, 1850-1980* focused particularly on the problem of the low economic growth rate of Britain since 1850.[5] Wiener argued that an important factor bearing on economic growth rates is the status of different occupations and in particular the status accorded to business, entrepreneurship and making money in contrast to that accorded to the professions like the law and medicine, and to the land and the life of the country gentleman. He argued that for various historical reasons business occupations have had low status in Britain and consequently the most ambitious and able young men have tended to make their careers in the professions. Those who have made money in business have sought to establish themselves as country gentlemen and encouraged their sons to enter the professions, so that the businesses which they originally built up have tended to stagnate. Wiener's theory has attracted a good deal of attention in Britain and is widely regarded as containing an important element of truth, but it applies much more widely than simply to Britain as an isolated case study and it is not implausible that the social standing of business may be an important factor generally in national rates of economic growth.

We turn now to the results of the study. All of the four psychological motives and values – the work ethic, competitiveness, achievement motivation and Wiener's status of the land-owner – were measured in the student samples in the 43 countries. Two of the countries, Transkei and the United Arab Emirates, were dropped from the main analysis because of their anomalous standings with regard to status as an independent state in the case of Transkei and the exceptional oil-rich nature of the economy in the case of the United Arab Emirates, thereby giving a sample of 41 countries.

When correlations were run between the four major psychological explanatory variables – the work ethic, achievement motivation, competitiveness and valuation of occupation of country landowner and farmer – and rates of economic growth on the 41 nation

15

sample, results were quite clear cut. Only competitiveness showed a positive association with rates of economic growth. The correlation was +0.59 across the nations as a whole. When the nations were divided into the two sub-groups of the affluent or economically developed and the less affluent or economically developing, the positive correlations of growth rates with competitiveness remained high and positive within each sub-group at +0.53 and +0.59 respectively.

One of the most striking features of the results is the high levels of competitiveness in the five 'miracle' economies of East Asia as contrasted with those in Europe. Set out below are the scores of the East Asian and the developed European countries on the competitiveness scale, shown in more detail later in *Table 11*.

Korea	13.66
Taiwan	13.39
Hong Kong	12.64
Japan	12.21
Singapore	11.38
Belgium	10.75
France	10.19
Britain	10.04
Norway	9.60
Germany	9.10
Sweden	9.05
Switzerland	8.99

It is clear that the East Asian and the European countries fall into two distinct groups with competitiveness levels substantially higher in the Pacific Rim.

In addition to competitiveness, a positive valuation of money was also found to be significantly related to economic growth rates in the set of nations as a whole and in the two subsets. This positive valuation of money was found to be highly correlated with competitiveness in the nations as a whole and in the two subsets, the correlations being 0.73, 0.83 and 0.51. The most straightforward explanation is probably that people who are highly competitive have a high valuation of money, probably because the possession of money constitutes a kind of status symbol which provides

16

gratification for strongly competitive individuals.

Tests were run on eight countries to determine whether competitiveness is correlated with a high valuation of money within countries as well as across countries. The method was to factor analyse the psychological measures. The results showed that in all eight countries competitiveness and high valuation for money combine to form a single factor which can be designated 'broad competitiveness'. The result shows that competitiveness and high valuation for money are closely associated in individuals as well as across countries. Across countries the correlation was 0.46. The association also held within the eight countries which were examined in detail, where the occupation of company director formed part of the broad competitiveness factor. In some of the Far Eastern nations, the occupation of small business owner also fell in this factor. The psychological mechanism is probably that competitiveness is the core trait, that highly competitive individuals will tend to direct their ambitions towards making money because they value it highly, and to entering the business occupations, because these are the occupations which yield good financial returns. Where the general level of competitiveness in a country is high, there would be relatively large numbers of individuals attaching high value to money and entering the business occupations, and this would contribute to the nation's rate of economic growth. The magnitude of the contribution of these psychological factors was calculated by multiple regression and yields a multiple correlation of 0.71, indicating that 50 per cent of the variance in rates of economic growth in the total sample of nations can be explained in terms of the level of broad competitiveness in the population.

Thus of the four psychological theories of economic growth – Weber's work ethic, Schumpeter's competitiveness, McClelland's achievement motivation and Wiener's valuation of the land – the results of the study support the Schumpeter thesis of competiveness and its expressions in high valuation of money and of the occupation of company director. When the nations were divided into the two subsets of the economically developed western capitalist economies and the developing nations, some slight support was found for Wiener's theory of the valuation attached to the occupation of country landowner as a negative influence on economic growth rates among the developed nations. However, the valuation attached to country living in the United Kingdom, for whose low rate of economic growth the theory was designed, was not uniquely high and was in fact rather lower than in the two more dynamic economies of the United States and Canada. There was also some slight support for achievement motivation as a factor among the economically developing nations. Nevertheless among these two subsets of nations the broad competitiveness factor appears to be the most important determinant of rates of economic growth.

There is therefore a temptation to conclude that among the theorists of the psychological contribution to economic growth, Schumpeter was the one who got it right. However, it has to be pointed out that the present study only tests the rival theories for the contemporary period. The results do not disconfirm Weber's theory that the Protestant work ethic was a significant factor in the development of capitalism in Northern Europe in the sixteenth and seventeenth centuries, McClelland's theory of the operation of achievement motivation in various historical periods, or Wiener's theory that the low social standing of business impaired economic growth in Britain from the late nineteenth century up to the early post World War Two decades. It is quite possible for factors which are significant determinants of economic growth in one historical period to cease to be significant determinants in another. For instance, the possession of good supplies of coal may have been a significant determinant of economic growth in nineteenth century Britain but makes little contribution to economic growth today. Nevertheless, the results of the study do indicate that of the four theories of the psychological contribution to economic growth, the only one substantiated by the data to any significant extent is Schumpeter's thesis of competitiveness.

2.   The work ethic in the post industrial society

The second question examined in the study concerns whether there is evidence for a decline in the strength of the work ethic in post industrial societies. The leading theorist on this issue is Daniel Bell whose influential book *The Coming of the Post Industrial Society* predicted that such a decline would occur.[6] Bell accepted the theory that the Protestant work ethic played a significant role in the economic growth of capitalist industrial societies. He argued that these are characterised primarily by the production of goods, but that these have begun to evolve and will continue to evolve further into 'post industrial societies' where the production of goods decreases and the selling of services becomes increasingly more important. There is no doubt that a tendency of this kind has taken place in recent decades in the most economically developed and affluent western economies.

However, Bell maintained further that the work ethic has declined in post industrial societies, and will continue to decline further and be replaced by an ethic of hedonism and leisure. Whether or not this is true has been difficult to determine. The belief that the work ethic has declined in the economically developed nations is certainly widespread. For instance, Katzell and Yankelovich reported a survey where 79 per cent of American managers believed that 'the nation's productivity is suffering because the traditional American work ethic has eroded',[7] but whether this belief is correct is less certain. The research literature on the question has been thoroughly reviewed by Furnham whose overall verdict is that there is no strong evidence for a decline in the strength of the work ethic in economically developed nations.[8]

There are two ways of obtaining evidence on whether the work ethic has declined in economically advanced or post industrial societies. Firstly, it would be possible to collect evidence on the strength of the work ethic over time in individual countries, taking comparable samples at two points in time and determining whether a secular decline has taken place. Curiously enough, it does not appear that a study of this kind has ever been done, and it may be that the results of the present study will serve as a baseline for future investigations to determine whether any secular changes in the work ethic or other work attitudes occurs in countries which move progressively into the post industrial phase.

The second approach is to collect evidence from a number of countries at different stages of economical development and examine whether there is any systematic tendency for the work ethic to be weaker among the most affluent. This is the strategy adopted in the present study and the results will tell us whether

19

there is any tendency for the strength of the work ethic or any other work attitudes to be weaker in the most advanced post industrial societies.

Bell's theory of the decline of the work ethic in post industrial societies was tested by running the correlation between the strength of the work ethic and per capita incomes. The results showed that the strength of the work ethic was correlated -0.15 with per capita Gross Domestic Product, a good proxy for incomes, across the 41 nations and among the economically developed nations the correlation was $+0.03$. Neither correlation is either substantial or statistically significant and therefore the results give no support to the thesis that the work ethic shows any tendency to decline in affluent post industrial societies.

The thesis can be subjected to an additional test. When the work attitude measures are factor analysed across countries there emerges a broad work commitment factor comprising the work ethic, mastery, achievement motivation and achievement via conformity. We can therefore ask whether this broader work commitment factor shows any tendency to decline in the high per capita income countries. The correlations between work commitment and per capita income across the 41 nations was -0.06, confirming that there is no tendency for work commitment to decline among the economically developed post industrial societies.

Nevertheless, the study does reveal some interesting trends associated with national per capita incomes. Among the nations as a whole per capita income is negatively correlated with competitiveness (-0.50), valuation of money (-0.61) and valuation of the occupation of company director (-0.27). These negative correlations are also present among the subset of economically developed nations, where the three correlations are -0.31, -0.46 and -0.48. Thus it appears that as nations become more affluent the populations become less competitive and the drive to acquire money and the attractiveness of the occupation of company director slackens. There is a complementary increase in the valuation of the caring professions of doctor, social worker and teacher, where the correlations with per capita income are $+0.29$, $+0.38$ and $+0.69$. Thus the results suggest that among the economically developed nations there is not so much a diminution of the strength of the work ethic or more broadly of work commitment with increasing affluence, as a redirection of the work ethic away from the drive to make money in business and towards the caring professions. No doubt many will welcome this result as a more satisfactory trend than the evolution of an ethic of hedonism and leisure predicted by a number of sociologists for the post industrial society.

The strategy of the study employed what has sometimes been called the 'shotgun design' in which measures of a number of different work attitudes were obtained and examined for possible relationships with economic growth and per capita income in the hope that one or two of the measures might strike the target and reveal interesting relationships. This kind of approach necessarily generates a lot of non-results which are rather uninteresting except in so far as they tend to falsify certain theories which predict that positive associations should exist. For this reason this opening chapter has been written in such a way that it can be read by readers who may wish to see a summary of the significant positive results of the investigation before turning, or not as the case may be, to the detailed presentation which constitutes the body of the book.

2   Psychological Factors in Economic Growth

It has long been believed that national rates of economic growth are to some degree determined by the attitudes to work of the population. This chapter describes the problem in broad terms and outlines the principal theories which have proposed that psychological attitudes make a significant contribution to economic growth.

1.   Economic growth and its causes

Economic growth consists of the increase of a nation's income from one year to another. A nation's income is the sum of the incomes of all its population. It can be measured as national income or as the value of gross domestic product or gross national product. Statistics for these measures are calculated each year by the United Nations Secretariat in Geneva and are published in the annual *Statistical Yearbooks* and *National Accounts Statistics*.

Historical statistics for the major developed economies are available since 1870 and are shown for 12 nations in *Table 1*. It will be

Table 1: Annual percentage rates of growth of output (GDP) in 12 countries at constant prices[9]

	1870-1913	1922-9	1929-37	1951-73
Belgium	2.0	3.4	0.1	4.1
Canada	3.8	6.2	-0.2	5.1
Denmark	3.2	2.6	1.9	3.9
France	1.6	4.4	-0.5	5.1
Germany	2.8	4.2	2.6	5.9
Italy	1.5	2.9	1.4	5.2
Japan	2.5	2.9	4.8	9.5
Netherlands	1.9	3.5	0.2	5.0
Norway	2.1	4.2	2.5	4.2
Sweden	2.8	5.0	2.2	3.8
UK	1.9	2.6	2.0	2.8
USA	4.1	3.3	-0.2	3.5

seen that some nations achieve consistently better growth rates than others over a long period of years. The growth rate of Japan has been exceptionally strong and in the post World War Two period has been about three times as great as that of the slower growing Western nations such as the UK and the USA.

National economic growth rates are largely reflections of increases in the productivity or productive efficiency of those in employment. Historical figures for the growth of productivity in the major industrialised nations have been compiled by Madison and are shown in *Table 2*. As will be seen, Japan has achieved the greatest gains in productivity while the lowest gains have been in the UK and the USA.

Table 2: Phases of Productivity Growth (GDP per Man Hour) 1870-1976

	annual average compound growth rates					
	1870-1913	1913-50	1950-76	1950-60	1960-70	1970-76
Australia	0.9	1.4	2.8	2.8	2.4	3.3
Austria	2.1	0.8	5.7	5.9	5.9	5.0
Belgium	1.2	1.5	4.5	3.1	5.0	6.1
Canada	2.0	2.3	2.8	3.1	2.8	2.3
Denmark	1.9	1.7	4.0	3.0	5.1	3.1
Finland	1.8	1.9	5.0	4.1	6.8	3.6
France	1.8	1.7	4.9	4.4	5.3	5.0
Germany	1.9	1.2	5.8	6.8	5.4	4.7
Italy	1.2	1.8	5.3	4.3	6.5	5.0
Japan	1.8	1.4	7.5	5.8	10.1	6.1
Netherlands	1.2	1.5	4.1	3.5	4.7	4.1
Norway	1.6	2.5	4.4	4.1	5.2	3.6
Sweden	2.4	2.9	3.8	3.5	4.8	2.7
Switzerland	1.5	1.9	3.4	3.5	4.0	2.3
UK	1.1	1.5	2.8	2.3	3.3	2.8
USA	2.1	2.5	2.3	2.4	2.5	1.8
Average	1.7	1.8	4.3	3.9	5.0	3.8

The growth of national productive efficiency is undoubtedly determined by a number of factors. Economists have been able to identify the major economic variables, of which the five generally regarded as the most important are these:

(a) *The strength and stability of demand.* Where demand for goods and services is low there will be high unemployment and hence the same labour will not be productively employed. This occurred in many countries during the 1930s and again in the 1980s when high unemployment led to considerable losses of output. This in turn came through as a slackening of the rate of economic growth.

(b) *The rate of technical progress.* Goods and services are constantly subject to technical improvements which raise the productivity of workers. Throughout most of the present century the United States has been the leading country in technical innovation and other countries have tended to adopt American advances. In general it is easier to borrow technical innovations than to pioneer them and this is a major reason why American productivity and economic growth have been generally lower than in other economically advanced countries. In the 1980s Europe and Japan caught up with the United States in productivity levels and began to become technical innovators. The Japanese took the lead in television and video-recorder technology and Britain and France in supersonic aircraft represented by Concorde. It is probable that economic growth and productivity rates will slow in Japan and Europe when they can no longer adopt American advances and are forced to become technical innovators themselves.

(c) *Growth and level of capital stock.* Labour productivity is heavily dependent on the quality of machinery and other elements of capital stock and will reflect the rate at which these are introduced.

(d) *International diffusion mechanisms.* Countries can often learn about efficient productivity practices from other countries. This is done through trade and other channels of communication.

(e) *Structural changes in employment.* There have been two principal changes in employment patterns during the last century. The first has been the shift of large numbers of people from agriculture to manufacturing and the second the shift out of manufacturing and into services. These shifts have taken place from less productive to more productive occupations and hence have generated increases in productivity.

While these factors are capable of providing partial explanations of growth in productivity and incomes they have not been found sufficient to provide a complete explanation for economic growth. There remains a residual which economists have attributed to a variety of psychological and sociological qualities in the population. Two types of explanations have been advanced. Firstly, it has frequently been posited that human skills developed by education are a significant factor in national rates of economic growth. The classical statement of this theory was made by Denison who promoted the thesis that education constituted an investment in 'human capital',[11] analogous to the investment in the physical capital of plant and machinery. This theory enjoyed considerable assent in the late 1960s and 1970s and provided intellectual authority in many countries for the expansion of education. However the case has been difficult to establish beyond doubt. Education is undoubtedly associated with earnings among individuals in the sense that those with university education earn more than those without,[12] but it is not easy to show conclusively that education is responsible for the development of economically remunerative skills. The counter argument is that those who obtain university education tend to have other advantages of home background and intelligence which are the crucial factors responsible for their higher earnings. This problem has proved impossible to resolve to the satisfaction of sceptics of the thesis that education contributes to economic growth.

The second type of non-economic factor advanced to explain economic growth consists of people's motivations. In general terms this thesis is reasonable. The innovations on which economic growth depends are made by individuals who need to have the motivation to make these innovations. The problem is to identify the nature of the relevant motivations. The leading figures who have made contributions to this problem are Max Weber, J A Schumpeter, D C McClelland and M J Wiener. We must turn now to give an outline of the work of these writers.

2. Max Weber and the Protestant work ethic

The first important statement of the role of psychological factors in economic growth appeared in 1904 with the publication of Max Weber's *The Protestant Ethic and the Spirit of Capitalism*.[13] Up to this time economists had emphasised the operation of economic variables in economic growth but in this book Weber maintained that Protestant beliefs were the crucial factor in the rapid development of capitalism in the sixteenth and seventeenth centuries. The essential feature of Protestantism, according to Weber's thesis, was a belief in hard work as a moral value. More broadly, there was a syndrome of Protestant beliefs consisting of the avoidance of idleness and waste in any form, the deferment of immediate rewards and pleasures, saving of surplus wealth and man's religious obligation to do his best at whatever occupation God had assigned him in life. These beliefs were preached by Luther and Calvin and the precepts were widely followed by the new Protestants who accepted their teachings.

The Protestant work ethic attained its most vigorous expression in the teaching of Calvin. Part of this teaching consisted of the doctrine of predestination, in which it was held that God had already chosen the elect. These would go to heaven while those not chosen were damned. It was further believed that an individual could demonstrate that he belonged to the elect by his success in his occupation..Hence in addition to the emphasis on hard work as a moral duty, Calvinists were additionally motivated to achieve success in this world as a sign that they were members of the elect and not destined for damnation. Thus among Calvinists an element of fear was added to the ethic of hard work as a moral obligation.

The potency of this belief structure – the Protestant work ethic – as an engine of capitalism is the more persuasive when it is set against the contrasting values of Catholicism. In the mediaeval and renaissance Catholic Church the prescribed ideal way of life was one of poverty and self-abnegation. The ideals were those of retreat from the world to a life of prayer in the monastery, of the propertyless mendicant friar, or of serving the poor after the manner of St Francis of Assisi and divesting oneself of the taint of wealth. The Catholic Church was in general not merely indifferent to capitalist enterprise but actively hostile to it in a variety of ways. Among these was the treatment of the lending of money with interest, an important facility for a capitalist economy, as a mortal sin, the sin of usury, and punishable by eternal damnation. Thus in the Protestant Reformation the generally unsympathetic views of the Catholic Church were transformed into a belief structure highly favourable to capitalist enterprise.

The credibility of Weber's thesis rests on three principal considerations. First, there is the intrinsic persuasiveness of the proposition that Protestant people brought up to believe in the moral duty of hard work and that worldly success is a sign of salvation in the next world, are probably going to work harder than Catholic people brought up to believe in the superiority of a life of poverty and withdrawal from the world. Secondly, there is the consideration that once the Reformation was under way the Protestant countries of Germany, the Netherlands, Switzerland, England and Scandinavia began to pull ahead of the Catholic countries in terms of technological innovation and economic growth. The strongest contrasts lie in the steady decline of Spain, the leading power of sixteenth century Europe, and of Portugal, a great maritime and trading nation. The decline of Italy was less marked but nevertheless real, since the city states of North Italy were the world centres of commerce and industry in the fourteenth, fifteenth and early sixteenth centuries. Only Catholic France and Belgium stood as partial exceptions to the emergence of the Protestant nations as the leading enterprise cultures. The divergence between the Catholic and Protestant nations in Europe also occurred in the new world. Here the dynamic capitalist economies of the predominantly Protestant United States and Canada present a striking contrast with the sluggish economies of the Catholic nations of South and Central America.

The third strand of evidence in support of Weber's thesis is that even within Catholic countries the most economically enterprising minorities and individuals tended to be Protestants. Among minorities the best known are probably the French Huguenots, of whom H A L Fisher wrote that 'in commerce and maritime adventure, as well as in all branches of industry such as weaving of silk, which in that age demanded a high measure of technical skill, these Protestant Frenchmen out-distanced their Catholic fellow citizens'.[14] Louis XIV expelled them from France in 1685 by his Edict of Nantes and they transferred both themselves and their valuable commercial skills and attitudes to England and other Protestant countries.

Similarly, at the level of the individual, historical research has established that almost all the great entrepreneurs and financiers of the Counter-Reformation were Protestants and many of them Calvinists. This was true even in the Catholic countries. Cardinal Richelieu in France relied on Calvinist bankers, the Rambouillets and Tallemants; the Catholic Habsburgs in Austria were largely financed by Hans de Witte, a Calvinist from Antwerp; and even in Madrid, Philip IV maintained his armies through the good offices of François Grenus, a Swiss Calvinist from Berne. It is a remarkable tribute to Weber's thesis that subsequent historical research should have confirmed in detail the contribution made by Calvinists to the progress of European capitalism in the seventeenth century. Trevor Roper has reviewed the historical research on this question and concluded that 'there is a solid ... core of truth in Weber's thesis'.[15]

Weber's theory attracted considerable interest as soon as it was published and this interest has continued right up to the present day. Among the enormous volume of commentary on the theory there have naturally been criticisms, but for the most part these have been based on misunderstandings of the theory. W H Tawney marshalled the evidence that there was a flourishing capitalist culture in the Catholic city states of North Italy in the fourteenth and fifteenth centuries and this has sometimes been taken to show that Weber has been disproved.[16] But of course this is not the case. Weber never maintained that capitalist enterprise could only be carried out by Protestants. His position was only that the Protestant belief structure was peculiarly conducive to the development of a vigorous capitalist economy. He recognised that other psychological motives could also generate capitalist enterprise. Indeed, he explicitly stated that once the fervour of Reformation Protestantism had abated, other motives such as the pursuit of wealth, the establishment of a family dynasty and so forth continued to be sufficient to maintain the momentum of economic progress in Protestant nations.

It is worth noting that Weber's thesis was not primarily a theory about the entrepreneur, the prime mover in the enterprise culture. The Protestant work ethic coloured the work attitudes of all individuals who subscribed to the belief. Most of these would be employees and subsistence small farmers, although it also affected and motivated entrepreneurs. Nevertheless, the major psychological effect of the Protestant work ethic was to introduce a high level of professionalism and commitment to work throughout society, not merely in the minority of entrepreneurs.

While Weber's thesis has generated a great deal of work in a variety of fields, perhaps the most important has been the construction in recent years of questionnaires for the measurement of the work ethic in individuals. One of the best of these was published by Mirels and Garrett.[17] This questionnaire consists of a set of 19 questions of the type 'There are few satisfactions equal to the realisation that one has done his best at a job' and 'People who fail at a job usually have not tried hard enough'. The questionnaire yields a score and this is a measure of the strength of the individual's work ethic. Studies using this questionnaire have shown that people who score highly work harder and longer at tasks of various kinds than those who score low. Thus recent work has provided direct confirmation of the validity of the Weber thesis at the level of the individual and shown that the strength of the Protestant work ethic is still a powerful determinant of effort and commitment.

There have also been other interesting results arising from the use of questionnaires of this type. For instance, it appears to be no longer the case that Protestants score higher on work ethic values than Catholics in the United States. The work ethic as a peculiarly Protestant value has apparently declined. For this reason some workers in recent years have dropped the prefix Protestant and write only of the work ethic.

At the level of individuals it has been shown that those with high work ethic scores enjoy greater satisfaction at their jobs and have higher morale in addition to putting more effort into the performance of dull routine tasks.[18] In terms of scientific methodology, such results as these can be regarded as verified predictions from Weber's thesis.

It would be difficult to overestimate the signficance of Max Weber's pioneering work on the Protestant work ethic. He was the first to establish firmly the importance of psychological determinants of economic growth and the enterprise culture. The book had a profound influence on those who subsequently took up this question and these included not only sociologists and psychologists but also economists, of whom the first was J A Schumpeter, to whose work we now turn.

3.   J A Schumpeter: the entrepreneur as innovator

It is generally considered that the first economist to acknowledge and analyse the psychology of the entrepreneur as the prime mover in economic growth was J A Schumpeter whose discussion of this question was published in *The Theory of Economic Development*.[19] Hitherto economists had largely followed Adam Smith and Karl Marx who, in spite of their considerable differences, both assumed that there was everywhere an adequate supply of rational economic men motivated to make money and that this was sufficient, so far as psychological motivation was concerned, to fuel economic development.

Schumpeter disputed this assumption. His basic point was that individual entrepreneurs were the key element in the introduction of the improvements in business methods, organisation and technology which themselves underlie economic growth. An adequate supply of efficient innovating entrepreneurs cannot be taken for granted and is by no means universally present in all societies. To understand economic progress Schumpeter therefore thought it necessary to analyse the psychology of the entrepreneur. To this question he made three important contributions, namely those concerning the characteristics of the entrepreneur, the functions in the economy that the entrepreneur performs, and the nature of the psychological motivations that drive the entrepreneur. So far as characteristics of the entrepreneur are concerned, Schumpeter considered that he has a statistically highly unusual set of abilities and attributes. Schumpeter had in mind here what might be called the heroic entrepreneur of the grand enterprise and not the small individual who sets up his own one-man window cleaning business. It is doubtful whether Schumpeter would have argued that the abilities required for such small scale entrepreneurship are particularly unusual.

The attributes of the heroic entrepreneur, as described by Schumpeter, consist of a special intuitional capacity to see things in a way that afterwards proves correct – new and more efficient forms of organisation, production, improved products which will command a market. In terms of contemporary psychology this ability would be considered a function of creativity and high intelligence. In addition the entrepreneur requires exceptional energy and the capacity to withstand the social opposition which is normally incurred by anyone who upsets traditional practices. Each of these characteristics is itself fairly uncommon, but the necessary combination of all of them in a single individual greatly increases the rarity of individuals possessing the full spectrum of abilities and personality qualities required for successful entrepreneurship.

Schumpeter turned next to the economic functions performed by the entrepreneur. He considered that these were essentially concerned with innovations and that these generally consisted of the introduction of new combinations of processes. He identified five types of these innovations: the introduction of a new product or service, with which potential customers are not yet familiar; the introduction of a new method of production, not yet tested in the particular branch of manufacture; the opening of a new market into which that particular product or service had not previously entered; the use of a new source of supply of raw materials or half-manufactured goods; introducing a new organisation in an industry such as the breaking up of a monopoly or cartel, or alternatively creating a monopoly or cartel position.

Schumpeter's third major contribution was concerned with the psychological motivation of the entrepreneur. He considered that three motives were most prominent and described these as follows. First, there is 'the will to found a private kingdom, and usually, though not necessarily, a dynasty'. He likened the drive as an attempt to achieve something like the position of the feudal baron who enjoyed power, status and independence in his domain and could contemplate his barony passing down through future generations of his family. The motive should more properly be considered a group of motives with a common core and can range from what Schumpeter described as spiritual ambition to mere snobbery.

The second motive for entrepreneurship is 'the will to conquer: the impulse to fight, to prove oneself superior to others, to succeed for the sake, not of the the fruits of success, but of success itself'. Schumpeter considered this drive an expression of the same motive as underlies the playing of games. Just as people play games like chess, bridge, scrabble and so on simply for the sheer pleasure of

31

pitting their wits against others and, hopefully, winning, so many entrepreneurs are motivated by the drive to win in the game of life itself. The financial gains are then an index of success, rather like the few pounds the bridge player might collect after an evening of successful rubbers. The bridge player does not play to make the money, but the money won is a symbol of success.

Thirdly, entrepreneurs are commonly motivated by 'the joy of creating'. What Schumpeter seems to envisage here is a canalisation of the creative drive of the scientist, writer and artist into the world of business. Unlike the first two motives the creative drive has no competitive element. The satisfaction is derived from building something satisfying, like a child building a tower with a set of bricks.

The critics of Schumpeter's work on the entrepreneur may complain that it is merely impressionistic and what is sometimes called 'armchair theorising'. Nevertheless, it has considerable intuitive appeal and provides a far more comprehensive analysis of entrepreneurship than was given by Weber.

4. David C McClelland: achievement motivation and economic growth

In spite of the pioneering work on the psychology of the entrepreneur of Weber and Schumpeter it was some time before psychologists took up this problem. The first to do so was David McClelland and the group he assembled at Harvard in the 1950s. The results of their work appeared in 1961 in *The Achieving Society*.[20] To this day it remains the most comprehensive and ambitious attempt to construct a psychological theory of entrepreneurship and economic growth.

The key concept in McClelland's work is that of achievement motivation. This is defined as the motive to achieve a standard of excellence in an undertaking and satisfy an inner need for personal accomplishment. The motive necessarily has a competitive component because the achievement of excellence can only be judged against a norm of average standards of attainment. The achievement motive is not the same as Weber's Protestant work ethic, since it lacks the moralistic flavour of Weber's concept. It does however resemble Schumpeter's entrepreneurial motive for the attainment of success for its own sake.

McClelland considers the achievement motive as the key to the psychological motivation of the entrepreneur. Individuals with strong achievement motivation tend to make their careers in entrepreneurship because building up one's own company provides the most satisfactory conditions for the full satisfaction of the motive. The reason for this is that the entrepreneur receives unusually clear signals of the degree of his success or failure in the form of the existence and size of his company and the magnitude of its profits. In this respect the entrepreneur is quite unusual compared with many if not most occupations of modern life.

In bureaucratic organisations there is either no yardstick, or at best a poor one, with which to evaluate the quality of an individual's performance. But in the case of successful entrepreneurs, their achievement is there for all to see and is quantified by the annual profit statement. To employ Schumpeter's analogy, they are like the bridge player whose skill is displayed in the number of points he has accumulated by the end of the evening.

An important feature of McClelland's work was the development of a technique for the measurement of the strength of an individual's achievement motivation. This consisted of the so called projective test in which people are shown pictures and asked to write stories about them. It is considered that people will tend to betray their preoccupations, interests and values in the kinds of stories they write, just as it can reasonably be inferred that, say, Milton was preoccupied with religion or Proust with the distinctions of social class from the amount of attention they gave to these themes in their writing. In the case of McClelland's projective test, the stories can be assessed for the degree to which they are concerned with achievement and on this basis the individual writing the story is given a score.

Having constructed an instrument for the measurement of achievement motivation the next step was to test whether this motive is strong in entrepreneurs. Several studies have shown that this is the case and independent investigations in other countries as well as the United States have confirmed McClelland's claim. It has also been shown that individual's high in achievement motivation work harder at challenging tasks of various kinds.[21]

When the nature of achievement motivation is examined more closely it is found to consist of three elements. First, it has a component of risk taking. It is a commonly asserted truism that entrepreneurship involves risk taking but there has been little detailed consideration of what kind of risk taking is involved. One can see groups of men lurking around betting shops almost any day of the week throughout the length and breadth of Britain and these men are engaged in risk taking. Do they therefore have an unusual psychological aptitude which could be potentially channelled into socially valuable and job creating entrepreneurship? Probably not. McClelland's studies of risk taking have shown that individuals who are high in achievement motivation have risk taking propensities of a rather special kind. Such individuals only incur risks which are carefully calculated, moderate in odds and in situations where their own efforts can affect the outcome. These are the kinds of risks undertaken by the entrepreneur and should be distinguished from the uncalculated, long odds and sheer chance risks of the race horse punter of the betting shop or the roulette player of the casino.

In addition to this particular kind of calculated risk taking, the individual high on achievement motivation derives satisfaction from work where there is scope for innovation, personal responsbility for decision making, and knowledge of results of the success or failure of personal skill and effort. Once again these correlates of achievement motivation are empirically demonstrated in McClelland's work and not simply impressionistic description or surmise. What typically happens is that individuals with this syndrome of psychological needs – ie high achievement motivation together with its components of the enjoyment of calculated risk, innovation, personal responsibility and knowledge of results – start their working life as paid employees but come to realise during the course of time that they are not deriving satisfaction from their work. They ponder on why this should be and conclude that it is because they are working in some large organisation where their needs are unfulfilled. Then they come to the realisation that their needs can only be satisfied fully if they are working for themselves in their own business. When this diagnosis has been made such individuals are ready to quit their life as employees, remortgage their house and start a new life as an entrepreneur. An illuminating description of this sequence of psychological self discovery is given in a study of entrepreneurs by Collins, Moore and Unwalla in their book *The Enterprising Man.*[22]

Up to this point McClelland was working at the level of individual psychology, concerned with the conceptualisation, analysis and measurement of achievement motivation in individuals and demonstrating its central role in the motivation of the entrepreneur. His next step was to move to the level of society and enter the province of sociology. The work demonstrating the importance of high achievement motivation for individual entrepreneurs leads naturally to the thesis that where the average level of the achievement motive is high in a society, regarded simply as an aggregate of individuals, there will be relatively large numbers of entrepreneurs and entrepreneurially minded persons. This in turn will express itself in the various macro indices of a strong enterprise economy such as fast rates of economic growth and a high rate of formation of small businesses. Hence McClelland next turned his attention to determining whether a relationship could be demonstrated at the sociological level between the strength of achievement motivation in a society and its rate of economic growth.

There were two principal attacks on this problem. First, McClelland took four societies where the strength of the enterprise culture rose and then fell over time. In these cases he endeavoured to show that the rise and fall in the strength of the economy was preceded by a rise and fall in strength of achievement motivation. The four societies selected for these studies were classical Athens over the period 900-1000 BC, seventeenth century Spain, England from 1400-1830, and the United States from 1800-1950. The empirical problems were to obtain measures of the general level of achievement motivation in the populations of these societies and also measures of economic growth rates. The method adopted for the measurement of achievement motivation was to make assessments from samples of the literature. This employs the same rationale as was used for the measurement of achievement motivation in individuals, namely the assumption that people express their values in the kinds of themes they write about. By the use of this technique McClelland was able to quantify the strength of achievement motivation prevailing in the selected societies at different points in time. The results showed that in all four cases achievement motivation was high in the early years of the society's initial rise. For instance, in the initial stage of classical Athens the writer Hesiod was enjoining the virtues of competition between people for riches and success. Among later writers these preoccupations with achievement and success were absent.

The second variable requiring measurement was rates of economic growth and for this McClelland employed various indices, eg in the case of Athens the numbers and distribution of Athenian pottery finds at the various locations (Sicily, North Africa and so forth) with which Athenian merchants carried on trade in the classical period. For all four of the societies studied McClelland was able to demonstrate the same pattern consisting of initially high levels of achievement motivation, sustained for a century or so and then undergoing a diminution, followed in time by a strongly growing economy, stabilisation and subsequent decline in economic strength. The temporal sequences in which the initially high levels of achievement motivation precede in time the first take-off stage of strong economic growth while the later fall off in achievement motivation again presages the subsequent weakness of the economies are persuasive evidence that the causal effect is from the pyschological levels of motivation present in the population to the economic growth and later decline of the societies.

In addition to the historical studies of these four societies, McClelland also tested the achievement motivation theory among nations of the twentieth century. The method here was to test for correlations across countries between levels of achievement motivation and subsequent economic growth. Two data sets were obtained. Firstly, achievement motivation levels for 1925 were quantified for 23 nations from an assessment of the themes present in children's reading books. Economic growth rates for the succeeding quarter century (1925-50) were quantified by the use of Colin Clark's international units of per capita national income and by the per capita growth of electricity consumption. For both indices the predicted positive correlations between levels of achievement motivation and subsequent economic growth were obtained (the correlations equalled 0.25 and 0.53 respectively).

This result was replicated in the second data set. Here levels of national achievement motivation, again using children's readers, were assessed for 39 countries for the year 1950. Economic growth was indexed by the growth of electricity consumption for 1952-8. The correlation between the two variables was 0.43, so that again the predicted positive correlation was present and substantial.

The final aspect of McClelland's work reviewed here concerns the question of how national levels of achievement motivation can be raised. McClelland has made three contributions to this problem.

Firstly, it appears that the individual's achievement motivation is largely formed during childhood and is developed as a result of the style of upbringing adopted by the parents. McClelland and his students have made empirical studies of this question and examined the relationship between different styles of parents' child rearing and levels of achievement motivation in their children. The conclusion of these investigations is that children high in achievement motivation are produced by parents who emphasise a syndrome of values among which the most prominent are achievement, independence and personal responsibility for mastering problems. For instance, such parents stress that the child should strive to do well at school and in competitive games by his own efforts (achievement), make his own decisions about such things as how he spends his pocket money, what books he reads, television he watches and so forth (independence), and try hard to do things for himself without asking for help (personal responsibility). Thus these parents encourage and pressurise their children to do well, to stand on their own two feet and take personal responsibility for their own successes or failures.

The opposite style of parental child rearing trains the child in dependency. Here the parents put less emphasis on encouraging their children to do well and take personal responsibility and make decisions on the child's behalf. Thus there is a kind of dimension of parental styles of upbringing of which the essential features are the degree of training for independence and achievement vs training for dependency and non-achievement. The parent's position on this dimension is the determinant of the child's level of achievement motivation. Once more it should be noted that this conclusion is based on empirically derived data, obtained from interviews with parents in which they were asked about the degree to which they emphasised to their children the importance of doing well at school, taking personal responsibility for themselves, etc, relating this parental style of upbringing to measurement of the child's level of achievement motivation and demonstrating a statistically significant association between the two variables.

If McClelland's conclusions on the genesis of achievement motivation are accepted, it might seem to follow that the level of achievement motivation in society can best be raised by attempting to alter parental styles of child rearing and in some way encouraging parents to adopt stronger independence and responsibility training strategies. While this might be theoretically desirable, it is clear that governments would encounter considerable difficulties in attempting to bring about a change of this kind. McClelland has therefore in a later book *Motivating Economic Achievement* considered the question of how far achievement levels can be increased among adults.[23] This book describes a good deal of work, principally in India and other third world countries, which has consisted of giving short intensive courses to small entrepreneurs and managers designed to raise their levels of achievement motivation. These studies claim considerable success and apparently show that the individuals exposed to these courses frequently experience an increase in achievement motivation and subsequently become more entrepreneurial and innovative in their business activities. These claims appear plausible if the courses are considered as essentially inspirational, presenting examples of successful entrepreneurs, showing what others have done and what could relatively easily be achieved by the individuals to whom the courses are addressed.

The third and final question considered by McClelland concerns the problem of the broad sociological factors responsible for the increases and subsequent declines in achievement motivation which have so often occurred over time in various societies, eg in Athens of the classical period, in the city states of North Italy during the Renaissance, in England at the time of the Industrial

Revolution and so forth. But although he was fully conscious of the importance of this problem neither McClelland nor any of those who have worked on the theory have been able to make any progress with it. In a preface to a new edition of his book, written in 1976, McClelland reviews subsequent work on his theory and concludes that 'no one has yet discovered any external conditions which regularly or in the main produce high levels of achievement motivation in a group'.[24] This is an important question for those thinking about how government might attempt to raise the levels of achievement motivation in society but McClelland can offer no direct help on how this could be brought about.

My concluding observations on McClelland's work are that this is certainly the most ambitious and comprehensive theory of the role of psychological factors in economic growth. The theory covers a number of interrelated areas, of which the most important are the positive relationships between achievement motivation and entrepreneurship both in individuals and in societies and the analysis of the determinants of achievement motivation in parental strategies of child rearing. An important feature of the theory is that its propositions are all empirically grounded and in this respect it compares favourably with the speculative assertions of a non-empirical nature advanced by J A Schumpeter and some more recent economists who have strayed into this field. McClelland's theory is essentially a set of reasonably well established inductive generalisations, is open to further corroboration or potential falsification and yields predictions of which several have been confirmed by independent experts.[25]

5. M J Wiener and anti-business values

It was shown in *Table 1* that the rate of economic growth in Great Britain has been relatively low over much of the last century. In an endeavour to explain this, M J Wiener has advanced the theory that British social values have been profoundly hostile to business and the making of money.[26] His thesis is that the occupations which carried social prestige and approval were the professions and the country landowner. The effect of this has been that intelligent and energetic young people have tended to make their careers in the professions rather than in business and this has deprived British business of talent. Furthermore, those individuals who have been successful in business and made fortunes have tended to set themselves up as country gentlemen and allowed their business to deteriorate..They have sent their sons to public schools from which they have proceeded into the professions, while the running of the family business has been left in the hands of poor quality managers.

Five major social groups are identified which have been antipathetic to business. Firstly, there were the aristocracy and gentry. These enjoyed the highest social status. They were landowners and derived their incomes from the rents received from their tenant farmers. This class denigrated business and those who made their money in trade. Many examples of this attitude can be found in nineteenth century English novels such as those of Jane Austen, Mrs Gaskell and Anthony Trollope.

Secondly, those in the professions also looked down on business. The prestigious occupations have been the law, medicine, the army and navy, the church, the universities and the public schools. These were the preferred occupations of upwardly mobile young men and the younger sons of the landowning aristocracy and gentry.

Thirdly, from the closing decades of the nineteenth century an intelligentsia class developed consisting of writers, artists and some academics. Many of these held socialist convictions and they also denigrated business. John Ruskin was a forerunner of this group, advocating arts and crafts work in villages rather than the mass production of the factories in the industrialised cities. In the twentieth century this group became more numerous and included people like Bernard Shaw, Sydney and Beatrice Webb, and other Fabians. From the 1920s onwards leading intellectuals were denigrating the making of money, eg as 'a disgusting morbidity, one of those semi-criminal, semi-pathological propensities which one hands over with a shudder to the specialists in mental disease' (J M Keynes, the eminent economist). 'The career of money making, industry, business, profits or efficiency is a despicable life in which no sane and enlightened person should be engaged' (Noel Annan, Provost of King's College, Cambridge, and later of University College, London).

Fourthly, the Labour Party was hostile to business as the dynamo of capitalism. The Labour Party became a national force from the 1920s. Its message was that the capitalist system was both ineffi-cient and socially unjust, and in this view it had the support of the majority of the intelligentsia. The Party's objective was the nationalisation of the means of production, distribution and exchange, some of which was put into effect by the Labour Govern-ment of 1945-51 with the nationalisation of the railways, coal mines, electricity industry and health service. This social philosophy and economic programme further undermined the confidence, social standing and morale of those working in the business sector.

Fifthly, the Conservative Party was by no means fully supportive of business. The party was dominated by the aristocracy and landed gentry and by the professions and retained the paternalist and corporatist values of the nineteenth century. In support of this reading of Conservative Party values Wiener cites quotations from leading Conservative politicians, eg 'Toryism has always been a form of paternal socialism' (Harold Macmillan), 'We are not a party of unbridled, brutal capitalism' (Anthony Eden) and the description of the private enterprise profit motive as an 'ungodly and rapacious scramble for ill-gotten gains' (Quintin Hogg).

Thus the business community in Britain has been under attack from all sides and the effect of this has been to undermine the morale of those working in business and to deflect the most able young people from business careers. In advancing this theory Wiener relies on the historical method which essentially consists of giving numerous examples to establish the case. These are up to a point persuasive but the method is nevertheless open to three criticisms. Firstly, while the case is well made that there has been considerable antipathy towards business in Britain among the so-cial and intellectual elite, it is difficult to assess how far this has affected the values held by the majority of the population. There is a great wealth of ability in the middle and working classes and it is open to question whether these have been much influenced by the snobbish disdain for business among the aristocracy, the professions or the intelligentsia.

Secondly it is difficult to establish the degree to which the denigration of business by dominant social groups has been stronger in Britain than in other economically advanced nations. It is true that in the United States there has been no aristocracy to denigrate business; no major political party devoted to the destruction of capitalism; and the disparagement of business by the professions and the intelligentsia may not have been so strident as in Britain. However, the contrast between Britain and the United States is not particularly persuasive because economic growth in the United States has been about the same as that in Britain in the post World War Two decades. In both countries economic growth has been low as compared with that in the countries of continental Europe and in Japan. It is not immediately obvious that the same degree of hositility to business may not be present among the dominant social and political groups in these countries, or at least in some of them. For instance, France and Italy have had large Communist parties and a powerful Marxist intelligentsia implacably hostile to capitalism and to business, yet both France and Italy have achieved substantially higher rates of economic growth in the post World War Two decades than either Britain or the United States. What is required to test the Wiener theory is quantitative evidence on attitudes towards money and to careers in business from a number of countries to determine whether these really are more adverse in Britain than elsewhere.

Thirdly, if the Wiener theory is accepted, it is an open question whether it is applicable only to the case of Britain or whether there may be other countries similarly affected, or perhaps affected to a lesser degree. It is certainly not implausible that the social standing of business and the value attached to money in a country may have an effect on whether talented young people enter business careers, and this in turn could affect the national rate of economic growth. But the theory needs empirical testing.

3   The Design of the Study

The principal objective of the study was to find questionnaire measures for the personality and motivational traits which theoreticians have posited may underlie national rates of economic growth and get them administered in a large number of countries. It would then be possible to examine whether national differences in the personality and motivational traits show any relationship with rates of economic growth. The results could also be usefully examined to determine whether the psychological measures show any relationship to per capita national incomes and also whether they show any consistent sex differences.

1.   The countries

The first step was to find social scientists in a large number of countries who would be willing to administer the questionnaires. This was done through personal contacts and by searching through journals to find people who had published papers in this general area. These people were then written to, sent an explanation of the research project, and asked if they would be willing to participate. As might be expected, quite a lot of people declined for one reason or another to join the project, while some undertook to participate but in the event failed to deliver the results. In some cases the results were invalid for various reasons and had to be discarded. In the end valid results were obtained for 41 nations and these are listed in *Table 3*.

2.   The subjects

Ideally a study of this kind would obtain data from representative samples of the populations of the various countries. However to obtain samples of this kind would be enormously expensive and beyond the scope of the inquiry. The only feasible samples which could be tested reasonably easily were university students.

Accordingly each investigator was asked to obtain results for a minimum of 150 male and 150 female students drawn from across all faculties in their respective countries. Some investigators tested more than the minimum number while others failed to reach it or, in some cases, some of the subjects had to be rejected because their questionnaires were incomplete. In some of the larger countries two investigators collected results. This was the case in France, India, Japan, the United Kingdom and the United States. The number of subjects obtained in each country are shown in *Table 5*. It may be considered that students do not constitute adequately representative samples but the use of students is defensible. If there are national differences in work motivations they should be present throughout the populations and detectable in any subsample. Other investigators have employed the same methodology of taking measures of national psychological differences from population subsamples rather than representative samples. For instance, McClelland obtained his measures of national levels of achievement motivation from a content analysis of the themes in children's reading books used in schools.[27] These will reflect the value systems of the educational officials and head-teachers who are responsible for selecting these reading books, but the value systems of the educational officials and headteachers should reflect those of the nation as a whole. Similarly, Hofstede uses questionnaire results obtained from managers in a multi-national corporation to provide measures of national differences in attitudes and values.[28] It is considered that these are legitimate procedures and the use of student samples is equally valid.

3. The questionnaires

The questionnaires of personality and motivational traits related to work attitudes were taken from the English language literature. In English speaking countries the questionnaires could be used as they stand but in non-English speaking countries they required translation into the indigenous language. It was important to ensure that the translations were accurate and for this purpose the method of 'back translation' was employed. In this method the questionnaire is first translated into the new language, a different person then translates it back into English, and a third person then compares the final English version with the original English version. The two versions should be closely similar. Any discrepancies are examined and the distortions in the translations are traced and corrected.

The questionnaires measured the following traits:

(a) *Work Ethic*: Weber's classical concept of a moral commitment to work.

(b) *Achievement Motivation*: McClelland's concept of a need for excellence.

(c) *Mastery*: the need for mastery of problems and events.

(d) *Competitiveness*: the motive to be better than others.

(e) *Achievement via Conformity*: identification with the organisation and its success.

(f) *Money Beliefs*: the importance attached to money.

(g) *Attitude to Saving*: the importance attached to saving.

(h) *Occupational Preferences*: the strength of preference for a career in business as contrasted with the professions.

The questionnaire results are presented for the countries for males and females separately because of the intrinsic interest of the sex differences on some of the traits. In addition an overall mean is given for each country. The questionnaire data were collected over the years 1986 to 1989. In calculating means for the nations for the personality and motivational measures the means for males and females have been weighted equally. The reason for this is that males and females obtain different means on a number of the measures. Hence where national samples contained unequal numbers of males and females it would not be satisfactory simply to add these to give an overall mean and it was necessary to weight the sexes equally. It will be seen that there are a few missing values for some of the personality and motivation measures for some countries. These are due to errors of various kinds which crept into the administration or scoring of the tests for some measures in some of the countries.

4. Economic statistics

The first economic variable considered in the study was the national rates of economic growth. These fluctuate from year to year as a result of domestic factors peculiar to individual countries and hence to average out these yearly fluctuations it is necessary to take the mean for a number of years. The period taken for the study was 1970-1985. The terminal year of 1985 was taken as the last year for which a complete set of statistics for all the countries was available at the time of writing up the study.

In addition to rates of growth, the second economic variable to be considered was per capita income. Per capita income was taken for the year 1985 and is expressed as the per capita GDP (Gross Domestic Product) for each country in US dollars either at the exchange rate or in purchasing power equivalents. These economic statistics are set out in *Table 3* for the countries for which the questionnaire data on work attitudes were collected. Subsequent chapters deal with the results of the questionnaire measures obtained from the countries and the relationship of these to the national rates of economic growth and per capita incomes.

The results of the study are analysed in three stages. Firstly, the correlations between each of the psychological measures with rates of economic growth and per capita income are presented. Secondly, the total effect of the psychological measures on economic growth rates are analysed by multiple regression. Thirdly, the psychological measures are simplified by factor analysis by reduction to four broader measures and the relationship of these to rates of economic growth and per capita incomes examined. In Chapter 14 there are a number of factor analyses of the work attitudes measures within countries and it is shown that the same factors are present within countries as are obtained across countries.

Table 3: National rates of economic growth and per capita incomes for the nations participating in the study

Country	Growth (1970-1985)	GDP($) (1985)
Argentina	1.3	2157
Australia	3.1	10666
Bangladesh	4.2	170
Belgium	2.5	7985
Brazil	6.3	1673
Bulgaria	4.9	1416h
Canada	4.0	13698
Chile	1.5	1329
China	7.3	227
Colombia	4.6	1191
Egypt	7.1	1365
France	2.9	9343
Germany	2.3	10266
Greece	3.5	3382
Hong Kong	8.4	6162
Iceland	4.3	10959
India	3.8	259
Iraq	6.5	2942
Ireland	3.7	5098
Israel	4.4	5776
Japan	4.5	10975
Jordan	5.2	1157
Korea	8.4	2089
Mexico	4.8	2247
New Zealand	2.6	6741
Norway	4.3	14092
Poland	3.8	2302h
Portugal	3.7	2026
Romania	7.0	1467h
Singapore	8.3	6843
South Africa	2.5	1693
Spain	3.1	4262
Sweden	2.0	12003
Switzerland	1.4	14555
Syria	6.5	1929
Taiwan	7.8g	4744f
Turkey	4.8	1069
UAE	25.3	20408
UK	2.1	8069
USA	2.7	16636
Venezuela	2.2	2864
Yugoslavia	4.2	1911

(a = 1981, b = 1982, c = 1983, d = 1984, e = 1979, f = 1987, g = 1973-87).
Sources: United Nations National Accounts Statistics and Statistical Yearbooks.

4   The Work Ethic

The work ethic was historically the first psychological motive identified as a possible factor in economic growth. The strength of the work ethic was advanced by Weber as a significant factor in the rise to economic power of the Protestant nations of Northern Europe from the seventeenth century onwards.[29] In subsequent decades several psychologists have constructed questionnaires to measure the strength of the work ethic in individuals as a means of obtaining quantitative data on the construct.

The questionnaire selected for use in the present study was constructed by Spence and Helmreich at the University of Texas.[30] It consists of six questions, the first of which runs 'It is important for me to do my work as well as I can even if it isn't popular with my co-workers'. Each question is answered on a 5 point scale running from 'strongly agree' (scored 4) to 'strongly disagree' (scored 0). The responses are totalled to give a possible maximum of 24.

The methodology usually adopted for the construction of a personality trait or motive is that the psychologist first writes out a number of questions believed to measure various aspects of the trait. These are then administered to a group of subjects and analysed statistically by factor analysis.

This procedure was carried out by Spence and Helmreich for their work ethic questionnaire. The factor analysis will normally show a general factor with which most of the questions are correlated. Normally questions with correlations above 0.3 are considered acceptable measures of the factor and can be used for the questionnaire. Spence and Helmreich have reported mean scores for male and female American college students, varsity athletes, business people and academic psychologists and these are shown in *Table 4*. It will be seen that there is a tendency for females to score a little higher than males in three of these samples. Spence and Helmreich do not report the numbers of subjects or the standard deviations and so the statistical signficance of these sex differences cannot be evaluated.

Table 4: Mean scores of males and females on the Spence-Helmreich Work Ethic Scale

	Males	Females
College students	19.8	20.3
College athletes	21.2	21.9
Academic psychologists	21.1	21.9
Business persons	21.1	20.7

In further studies Spence and Helmreich have found that the strength of the work ethic in university students is positively and significantly associated with their academic achievement assessed by grade point averages during the year following the taking of the work ethic test. However, there was no association between the work ethic and Scholastic Aptitude Test (SAT) scores, which can be taken as a measure of ability or intelligence, although SAT scores are also positively associated with academic achievement. Hence academic achievement appears to be a function of ability plus work ethic, which are themselves independent of one another. The same positive association between work ethic and achievement has been found for businessmen, using income as a criterion of achievement, and among academic scientists for whom achievement was measured by their citation index, ie the number of times their work is cited in the publications of other scientists. There is therefore quite strong evidence for the validity of the work ethic questionnaire, ie that it is positively associated with achievement and independent of ability.

The results of the study for the Work Ethic questionnaire are shown in *Table 5*. This gives first the total number of subjects for each country and the mean score weighting both sexes equally. The standard deviations are given in brackets. On the right of the table are given the means for males and females separately. The statistical significance of the differences between males and females was tested for each country by t tests and statistically significant differences are designated by asterisks. The sex differences provide a useful check on the reliability of the measures because there should

Table 5: Means and standard deviations for the Spence-Helmriech Work Ethic Scale

Country	Number	Total	Males	Females
Argentina	200	21.29(2.30)	21.23(2.39)	21.35(2.22)
Australia	297	19.57(2.80)	18.92(3.07)	20.21(2.52)***
Bangladesh	378	17.71(4.88)	19.44(3.70)	15.98(3.06)***
Belgium	300	18.55(2.50)	18.44(2.58)	18.66(2.42)
Brazil	306	21.06(2.50)	20.95(2.51)	21.17(2.49)
Bulgaria	291	19.72(3.53)	19.03(4.01)	20.36(3.04)**
Canada	164	19.96(2.60)	19.51(2.96)	20.41(2.23)*
Chile	265	20.59(2.49)	20.89(2.24)	20.29(2.73)
China	334	18.21(3.46)	18.32(3.35)	18.09(3.57)
Colombia	300	21.15(2.38)	20.95(2.46)	21.35(2.28)
Egypt	324	21.89(2.58)	21.45(3.03)	22.33(2.13)**
France	697	18.76(3.35)	18.32(3.83)	19.19(2.87)**
Germany	306	17.82(3.22)	17.46(3.52)	18.17(2.92)
Greece	311	20.57(2.39)	20.72(2.32)	20.42(2.46)
Hong Kong	306	17.30(3.26)	17.19(3.37)	17.40(3.14)
Iceland	320	20.31(2.27)	20.11(2.25)	20.51(2.29)
India	388	18.57(3.42)	18.55(3.26)	18.59(3.57)
Iraq	435	19.12(3.33)	18.67(3.33)	19.57(3.33)**
Ireland	300	19.23(3.24)	19.06(3.23)	19.40(3.24)
Israel	131	20.06(2.82)	19.79(2.99)	20.33(2.64)
Japan	403	16.67(3.07)	16.21(3.32)	17.12(2.82)**
Jordan	300	19.01(2.75)	18.99(2.66)	19.04(2.85)
Korea	317	20.49(2.57)	20.69(2.27)	20.29(2.87)
Mexico	417	21.29(2.46)	21.22(2.51)	21.35(2.41)
New Zealand	373	19.04(3.08)	18.99(2.94)	19.09(3.22)
Norway	126	19.65(3.01)	20.11(3.01)	19.18(3.01)
Poland	300	18.81(3.00)	18.51(3.24)	19.11(2.75)
Portugal	145	21.27(1.58)	21.13(1.59)	21.13(1.56)
Romania	300	20.54(2.86)	20.41(2.95)	20.66(2.77)
Singapore	458	19.85(2.39)	19.83(2.40)	19.87(2.73)
South Africa	898	19.42(3.57)	19.44(3.68)	19.40(3.46)
Spain	375	19.46(2.81)	19.40(2.88)	19.52(2.74)
Sweden	225	19.75(2.74)	19.45(2.96)	20.05(2.52)
Switzerland	237	18.61(2.68)	18.19(2.82)	19.03(2.53)*
Syria	300	18.05(2.66)	17.86(2.65)	18.24(2.67)
Taiwan	321	19.45(2.86)	19.33(3.07)	19.57(2.65)
Transkei	302	19.68(3.02)	19.47(3.08)	19.88(2.96)
Turkey	309	17.16(3.14)	16.67(3.20)	17.64(3.08)**
UAE	250	19.99(2.50)	19.98(2.56)	20.00(2.43)
UK	596	19.22(3.27)	18.74(3.66)	19.70(2.88)***
USA	684	20.52(2.44)	20.24(2.55)	20.79(2.33)**
Venezuela	278	21.86(2.60)	21.46(2.60)	22.25(2.60)*
Yugoslavia	334	19.53(2.98)	19.03(3.36)	20.03(2.61)**
Mean		19.55(2.84)	19.41(2.94)	19.70(2.74)

Asterisks (1, 2 and 3) denote statistically significant sex differences respectively at the 5, 1 and .1 per cent levels determined by t tests.

be a high measure of consistency between the scores obtained for each country for the two sexes. In the case of the work ethic questionnaire results the correlation between scores of males and females across the 43 countries is +0.83. This is highly statistically significant and represents a strong degree of consistency between the scores obtained by males and females. The sex differences are also a subject of interest in themselves and are considered later in the chapter.

The possible relationship of the strength of the Work Ethic Scale to economic growth rates and per capita incomes was examined in four ways. Firstly, correlations were computed for the entire sample of countries with the exception of Transkei. The reason for this omission is that the economic data are not available for this country. Secondly, the United Arab Emirates is an exceptional case because of its very high per capita income and fast rate of economic growth which it obtains almost entirely from oil extraction and investments. The effect of this is likely to distort the relationship between the psychological and economic measures and it was therefore considered sensible to calculate the correlations after excluding the United Arab Emirates and hence on 41 nations. Thirdly the countries were divided into two groups of the more affluent and the less affluent. The more affluent or economically developed countries were those with per capita incomes of 3,000 US dollars and above and include the nations of Western Europe, North America, the Far East with the exception of Korea, and Australia and New Zealand. The United Arab Emirates were omitted from this group because of the exceptional nature of the economy. This group consists of 20 countries. The second group of less affluent or developing nations comprised the remaining 21 nations with per capita incomes of less than 3,000 US dollars and consisted of the countries of South and Central America, Eastern Europe, the near East, Africa, the Indian subcontinent and Korea. The reason for dividing the nations into these two subgroups is that relationships between the personality and attitude measures might be present among nations at one stage of economic development but not at the other. Computation of correlation coefficients for the two subgroups separately makes it possible to determine whether this is the case.

The correlations between the national means for the Work Ethic Scale for the total sample of 42 nations, for the 20 economically developed nations and for the 21 developing nations are shown in *Table 6*. It will be seen that there are no associations between work ethic and economic growth rates in any of the three samples. There is also no association between work ethic and per capita income for the set of nations as a whole or for the economically developed nations, but there is a significant correlation of 0.47 among the economically developing nations which does not suggest any obvious interpretation. The overall verdict of the results must be that national differences in work ethic make no contribution to rates of economic growth in the contemporary period. This conclusion is reinforced by the low level of the work ethic in Japan (the lowest in the entire set of nations) and Hong Kong, two of the countries with the highest rates of economic growth in the post World War Two period.

Table 6: Correlations between the Spence-Helmreich Work Ethic Scale, economic growth and per capita incomes (decimal points omitted)

	All Countries	**41 Countries**	**Developed Countries**	**Developing Countries**
Economic Growth	02	−06	−09	−15
Per capita Income	−11	−15	03	47**

Asterisks denote statistical signficance at the 1 per cent level.

Turning now to the sex differences in the strength of the work ethic, it has been noted that the initial work by Spence and Helmreich in the United States found a tendency towards higher mean scores in females.[31] This result is confirmed in the international data. In 13 countries females obtained significantly higher mean scores than males, ie in Australia, Bulgaria, Canada, Egypt, France, Iraq, Japan, Switzerland,Turkey, UK, USA, Venezuela and Yugoslavia. Typically the size of the higher female mean is about one third of a standard deviation. In a further 22 countries females obtained higher means which were not statistically significant. In the remaining eight countries males obtained higher means than females but in only one of these, Bangladesh, was the difference statistically signficant. There is no obvious pattern differentiating the majority of countries where females obtain higher means from those where the sex difference is reversed. For instance, the strikingly higher male mean in Bangladesh is not found in neighbouring India. The inconsistencies probably have to be attributed to sample errors, but the overall tendency of females to obtain higher means is unmistakable.

5   Achievement Motivation

The achievement motivation concept of McClelland[32] is the most widely researched of the psychological motives believed to contribute to economic growth. The core of the concept consists of the need to achieve excellence in the performance of tasks. A useful recent discussion of the concept is available in Furnham and Lewis.[33]

Achievement motivation was measured by the Ray-Lynn Achievement Motivation Scale. This is based on an earlier achievement motivation constructed by the writer in the 1960s.[34] In the 1970s Ray in Australia developed the scale and produced a 14 item questionnaire.[35] The first question runs 'Is being comfortable more important to you than getting ahead?' The questions are answered yes (3), not sure (2) or no (1) with half the questions being reversed, (ie scored no = 3, not sure = 2 and yes = 1) to control for possible bias in some subjects of responding positively to all questions. The questionnaire yields a possible maximum score of 42.

Ray presents norms for the scale for adult samples in Glasgow, London and Sydney. In all three samples males obtain higher mean scores than females by approximately one half of a standard deviation. The total number of subjects was 100 in Glasgow and in London and 95 in Sydney, and although Ray does not give the statistical significance of the sex difference it would certainly be significant on this number of subjects. Results are also given for 100 White South Africans. The mean for the English speakers was 35.1 (sd 5.0) and for the Afrikaans 35.6 (sd 4.1), a little higher than those obtained in Glasgow, London and Sydney. Ray reports validation data showing that scores on the scale have appreciable correlations with peer ratings of achievement motivation, success orientation and actual achievement.

The results of the study for the Achievement Motivation Scale are set out in *Table 7*, which gives the means for the nations

Table 7: Means and standard deviations for the Ray-Lynn Achievement Motivation Scale

Country	Total	Males	Females
Argentina	35.81(3.58)	36.12(3.29)	35.50(3.86)
Australia	32.57(4.88)	31.49(5.26)	33.65(4.50)***
Bangladesh	–	–	–
Belgium	33.52(3.96)	33.51(4.23)	33.53(3.69)
Brazil	36.73(3.48)	36.74(3.70)	36.72(3.26)
Bulgaria	32.24(4.44)	32.25(4.75)	32.22(4.12)
Canada	34.19(4.35)	33.90(4.64)	34.48(4.05)
Chile	29.30(2.93)	28.74(2.93)	29.06(2.92)
China	30.40(3.84)	31.11(3.84)	29.69(3.84)***
Colombia	36.24(3.71)	36.27(3.83)	36.21(3.59)
Egypt	34.44(4.77)	35.13(5.13)	35.75(4.41)**
France	32.09(4.46)	31.01(4.74)	33.16(4.18)***
Germany	28.79(5.19)	29.39(5.35)	28.81(4.98)
Greece	35.19(3.94)	35.47(3.94)	34.91(3.93)
Hong Kong	31.65(3.46)	31.75(3.30)	31.55(3.62)
Iceland	32.06(4.49)	32.50(4.38)	31.62(4.59)
India	32.37(4.14)	32.20(4.24)	32.53(4.04)
Iraq	33.82(4.27)	33.74(4.28)	33.89(4.25)
Ireland	31.92(5.04)	32.00(5.38)	31.84(4.70)
Israel	34.10(4.70)	34.59(4.43)	33.60(4.97)
Japan	29.69(4.63)	29.69(5.11)	29.69(4.15)
Jordan	35.10(3.66)	35.35(3.55)	34.85(3.77)
Korea	33.02(4.38)	33.47(4.11)	32.56(4.64)
Mexico	36.63(3.65)	36.60(3.82)	36.65(3.48)
New Zealand	32.27(5.18)	32.00(5.09)	32.54(5.26)
Norway	31.65(4.69)	31.70(4.79)	31.60(4.58)
Poland	31.42(4.32)	31.68(4.53)	31.16(4.11)
Portugal	34.08(4.03)	34.00(4.25)	34.16(3.81)
Romania	33.97(4.10)	33.97(4.27)	33.97(3.92)
Singapore	33.49(4.29)	33.89(4.05)	33.09(4.52)
South Africa	34.57(4.30)	34.25(4.35)	34.89(4.25)*
Spain	33.57(4.27)	33.69(4.53)	33.45(4.00)
Sweden	31.95(4.36)	31.53(4.50)	32.37(4.21)
Switzerland	32.22(4.51)	32.16(4.76)	32.28(4.25)
Syria	31.32(3.68)	32.92(3.47)	33.73(3.84)
Taiwan	33.55(4.29)	33.95(4.62)	33.14(3.96)
Transkei	36.26(3.06)	36.03(2.83)	36.49(3.29)
Turkey	33.30(4.27)	32.70(4.27)	33.89(4.26)*
UAE	34.39(4.15)	34.13(4.12)	34.64(4.17)
UK	31.86(5.51)	31.28(5.69)	32.43(5.32)*
USA	35.15(4.09)	34.67(4.23)	35.63(3.94)**
Venezuela	29.41(4.20)	28.87(4.20)	29.94(4.20)*
Yugoslavia	31.83(4.09)	31.22(4.43)	32.43(3.75)**
Mean	32.81(4.22)	33.04(4.32)	33.20(4.12)

Asterisks (1, 2 and 3) denote statistically significant sex differences respectively at the 5, 1 and .1 per cent levels determined by t tests.

weighting the sexes equally followed by the means for males and females separately. The correlation between the means for males and females across countries is 0.93. This is highly statistically significant and indicates a good reliability of the scale as assessed by the consistency between the sexes across the nations.

The correlations between the national achievement motivation means and economic growth and per capita incomes are shown in *Table 8*. It will be seen that there are no statistically significant correlations between achievement motivation means and rates of economic growth or per capita incomes.

Table 8: Correlations between the Ray-Lynn Achievement Motivation Scale, economic growth rates and per capita incomes (decimal points omitted)

	All Countries	41 Countries	Developed Countries	Developing Countries
Economic Growth	18	14	10	15
Per capita Income	−01	−07	−15	18

Examination of the sex differences in achievement motivation shows that females obtain significantly higher means than males in nine countries, namely Australia, Egypt, France, South Africa, Turkey, UK, USA, Venezuela, and Yugoslavia. The reverse pattern of a significantly higher mean in males was found only in China. The initial studies on achievement motivation in the United States found that males tended to obtain higher means than females and theories were proposed that males were subject to greater socialisation pressures for achievement and that females tended, in some cases to develop 'fear of success' through socialisation pressures to avoid success.[36] Later studies suggested that the apparent sex differences in achievement motivation may have arisen because of the nature of the test used in the earlier investigations, namely Thematic Aperception Pictures generally showing men in various roles.[37] The national differences showing few overall sex differences in the strength of achievement motivation and a tendency towards higher means in females in a number of countries including the United States suggest that the initial American studies showing higher means in males should probably be ascribed to methodological inadequacies.

6   Mastery

Because of the centrality of achievement motivation in psychological theories of economic growth, it was decided to use a further
questionnaire which appears closely related to the concept. This is
Spence and Helmreich's Mastery Scale.[38] The concept is the importance attached to mastering a problem and the questions used in
the scale appear to reflect a concern for excellence and hence to
measure much the same as achievement motivation. Thus, the first
question runs 'I would rather do something at which I feel confi-
dent and relaxed than something which is challenging and difficult'.
McClelland's trait of the drive to tackle and solve challenging problems is conceptually closely similar. The mastery trait consists of 8
questions answered on a 4 (strongly agree) to 0 (strongly disagree)
scale and the responses are totalled to give a possible maximum of 32.

Spence and Helmreich obtained mean scores of 19.3 and 18.0 for
male and female college students respectively. They also showed
that high scores are associated with academic achievement as measured by grade point averages. A positive association between high
scores and achievement was also found for 11-12 year olds, among
businessmen using salary as a criterion of achievement, and among
academic scientists using the citation index as the achievement
criterion.

The results of the study for the Mastery Scale are given in *Table
9*, which shows first the means for the nations weighting the sexes
equally followed by the means for males and females separately.
The correlation between the means for males and females across
countries is 0.88, is highly statistically significant and indicates a
high level of consistency between the scores of the two sexes across
the nations.

The correlations between the Mastery Scale and economic
growth and per capita incomes are shown in *Table 10*. As with the

Table 9: Means and standard deviations for the Spence-Helmreich Mastery Scale

Country	Total	Males	Females
Argentina	20.43(4.43)	20.83(4.42)	20.03(4.41)
Australia	18.10(4.64)	18.20(4.93)	17.99(4.35)
Bangladesh	17.33(4.55)	17.93(4.55)	16.74(4.55)**
Belgium	19.13(4.25)	19.73(4.02)	18.54(4.41)**
Brazil	21.29(3.95)	21.13(3.61)	21.44(4.28)
Bulgaria	16.46(4.17)	16.49(4.20)	16.43(4.13)
Canada	19.53(4.24)	19.27(4.28)	19.79(4.19)
Chile	19.70(3.85)	19.88(3.85)	19.51(3.85)
China	18.06(3.68)	18.64(3.96)	17.48(4.39)*
Colombia	21.50(3.70)	21.43(3.90)	21.56(4.04)
Egypt	20.10(4.75)	20.77(4.81)	19.43(4.68)*
France	18.32(4.75)	18.19(5.00)	18.45(4.49)
Germany	17.48(4.21)	17.89(4.07)	17.07(4.34)
Greece	20.07(4.60)	20.82(4.42)	19.32(4.77)**
Hong Kong	16.95(3.83)	17.27(4.32)	16.63(3.34)
Iceland	21.22(4.06)	21.71(3.94)	20.73(4.17)*
India	19.03(3.75)	18.60(3.71)	19.46(3.79)*
Iraq	17.62(4.37)	17.91(4.40)	17.33(4.33)
Ireland	17.75(4.46)	17.66(4.61)	17.83(4.30)
Israel	21.04(3.80)	21.35(3.83)	20.72(3.77)
Japan	17.01(4.30)	17.09(4.75)	16.93(3.84)
Jordan	18.70(4.45)	18.79(4.62)	18.61(4.28)
Korea	18.71(4.33)	19.11(4.11)	18.31(4.54)
Mexico	20.51(4.17)	20.68(~~4.12~~) 4.18	20.35(4.22)
New Zealand	18.49(4.11)	18.46(4.28)	18.51(3.93)
Norway	19.01(4.28)	19.41(4.21)	18.60(4.35)
Poland	17.24(4.74)	17.91(4.99)	16.56(4.48)*
Portugal	21.24(3.14)	22.00(3.27)	20.48(3.00)*
Romania	20.64(4.90)	21.14(4.90)	20.14(~~4.84~~) 4.89
Singapore	18.19(3.92)	18.56(3.81)	17.82(4.02)
South Africa	19.66(3.72)	19.23(4.63)	~~20.09(2.81)*~~ 18.95(4.13)
Spain	17.78(4.25)	18.04(4.25)	17.52(4.25)
Sweden	19.64(4.23)	19.55(4.11)	19.73(4.35)
Switzerland	18.54(3.84)	19.16(3.76)	17.92(3.91)*
Syria	18.64(3.67)	18.71(3.80)	18.57(3.54)
Taiwan	20.49(4.15)	20.89(4.02)	20.08(4.27)
Transkei	17.98(4.71)	18.83(4.42)	17.13(5.00)**
Turkey	18.41(3.79)	18.31(3.69)	18.50(3.88)
UAE	18.57(4.07)	19.27(3.89)	17.87(4.24)*
UK	17.54(4.81)	17.42(5.15)	17.65(4.47)
USA	19.46(3.84)	19.80(3.72)	19.12(3.95)*
Venezuela	22.09(3.80)	21.57(3.80)	22.61(3.80)*
Yugoslavia	18.28(4.50)	18.17(4.66)	18.38(4.33)
Mean	19.02(4.20)	19.25(4.23)	18.79(4.16)

Asterisks (1, 2 and 3) denote statistically significant sex differences respectively at the 5, 1 and .1 per cent levels determined by t tests.

previous motivational traits, the correlations are given for the whole sample of nations, the whole sample omitting the United Arab Emirates, and for the economically developed and developing nations as separate groups. It will be seen that there are no statistically significant correlations between the Mastery Scale and either economic growth rates or per capita incomes.

Table 10: Correlations between the Spence-Helmreich Mastery Scale, economic growth rates and per capita incomes (decimal points omitted)

	All Countries	41 Countries	Developed Countries	Developing Countries
Economic Growth	−09	−07	02	−26
Per capita Income	−16	−11	05	15

Because the Mastery Scale was used in the study since it was considered an additional measure of achievement motivation, it is of interest to consider the consistency of the two measures. The correlation across the nations is +0.16 and is not statistically significant. It is evident therefore that the assumption that the Mastery Scale would serve as an additional measure of achievement motivation was mistaken. However the Mastery Scale does correlate +0.74 with the Work Ethic Scale indicating that these two measures have a good deal in common. The degree to which some of the scales may be measuring the same underlying traits is analysed by factor analysis in Chapter 13.

The sex differences on the Mastery Scale show that males obtain significantly higher means than females in 12 countries, namely Bangladesh, Belgium, China, Egypt, Greece, Iceland, Poland, Portugal, Switzerland, Transkei, United Arab Emirates, and the United States. There are three countries in which females obtain higher means, namely India, South Africa and Venezuela. The overall tendency is for males to score slightly higher than females.

7   Competitiveness

Competitiveness can be defined as the drive to win against others and obtain some form of dominance over them through winning. The drive was identified by Schumpeter as one of the major motivations of the entrepreneur.Competitiveness was measured by the Spence and Helmreich Competitiveness Scale, a five item scale.[40] The first question runs 'I enjoy working in situations involving competition with others'. Each question is scored on a strongly agree (scored 4) to strongly disagree (scored 0) format, thus giving a possible maximum score of 20. The Spence and Helmreich work has found mean scores for Texas male and female college students to be 13.6 (males) and 12.2 (females). They also found that males scored higher than females among college athletes (15.7 vs 14.3), business-persons (14.6 vs 13.8) and academic psychologists (11.7 vs 11.1). This consistent sex difference could have a genetic basis, since in many species males compete more strongly than females for rank or territory.[41] Alternatively, it may well be that males tend to be socialised into becoming more competitive than females.

It would probably be thought on common sense grounds that competitiveness would act as a motivator for work effort and by this means contribute to achievement, as Schumpeter proposed. Spence and Helmreich found that high competitiveness was positively correlated with the importance students attached to pay and prospects for promotion in jobs, with correlations in the range of 0.28 to 0.45.

The results of the study for the Competitiveness Scale are set out in *Table 11*, which gives the means for the nations weighting the sexes equally followed by the means for males and females separately. The correlation between the means for males and females across countries is 0.91, indicating a highly reliable scale as assessed by the consistency between the sexes across the nations.

Table 11: Means and standard deviations for the Spence-Helmreich Competitiveness Scale

Country	Total	Males	Females
Argentina	8.51(4.41)	9.08(4.48)	7.93(4.35)*
Australia	11.42(3.99)	11.64(4.00)	11.19(3.98)
Bangladesh	14.25(3.32)	14.56(2.70)	13.94(3.42)*
Belgium	10.75(4.18)	11.47(4.06)	10.03(4.19)*
Brazil	11.17(4.12)	11.58(4.21)	10.75(4.03)
Bulgaria	12.33(4.39)	11.94(4.51)	12.71(4.27)
Canada	12.03(3.87)	13.18(3.89)	10.88(3.85)***
Chile	11.54(3.73)	11.53(3.64)	11.55(3.81)
China	12.37(3.08)	12.92(3.06)	11.81(3.10)***
Colombia	12.97(3.70)	13.49(3.12)	12.45(4.15)*
Egypt	15.66(3.33)	15.90(3.43)	15.41(3.22)
France	10.19(4.48)	10.44(5.13)	9.93(3.82)
Germany	9.10(4.20)	10.12(4.47)	8.07(3.92)***
Greece	13.83(3.83)	14.00(4.06)	13.65(3.60)
Hong Kong	12.64(3.14)	12.51(3.41)	12.77(2.86)
Iceland	12.99(3.88)	13.97(3.32)	12.01(3.84)***
India	14.48(3.15)	14.95(3.13)	14.01(3.16)**
Iraq	14.04(3.69)	13.66(3.57)	14.42(3.80)*
Ireland	10.99(4.13)	11.65(4.20)	10.33(4.05)**
Israel	11.59(3.93)	12.62(3.79)	10.55(4.07)**
Japan	12.21(3.28)	12.69(3.35)	11.73(3.20)**
Jordan	14.77(3.01)	15.13(2.96)	14.41(3.03)*
Korea	13.66(3.50)	13.43(3.39)	13.88(3.61)
Mexico	13.82(3.65)	14.22(3.43)	13.41(3.86)*
New Zealand	11.13(3.67)	11.50(3.69)	10.75(3.64)*
Norway	9.60(3.94)	8.92(3.98)	10.28(3.90)
Poland	12.00(4.03)	12.39(3.96)	11.61(4.10)
Portugal	11.94(3.56)	12.00(3.83)	11.88(3.28)
Romania	13.68(3.47)	13.67(3.61)	13.68(3.33)
Singapore	11.38(3.69)	11.50(3.75)	11.25(3.63)
South Africa	12.50(4.07)	12.99(4.30)	12.00(3.84)
Spain	10.45(4.24)	10.87(4.35)	10.03(4.12)
Sweden	9.05(4.17)	9.29(4.22)	8.81(4.11)
Switzerland	8.99(3.90)	9.54(4.27)	8.44(3.53)*
Syria	14.03(2.83)	13.87(2.74)	14.19(2.17)
Taiwan	13.39(3.10)	13.88(3.03)	12.89(3.16)**
Transkei	16.24(3.37)	15.96(3.64)	16.52(3.09)
Turkey	12.78(3.87)	12.91(4.19)	12.64(3.54)
UAE	14.35(3.53)	14.42(3.35)	14.27(3.70)
UK	10.64(4.40)	11.37(4.70)	9.90(4.09)***
USA	12.76(3.49)	13.65(3.51)	11.86(3.47)***
Venezuela	10.99(4.20)	11.18(4.20)	10.80(4.20)
Yugoslavia	11.23(4.22)	11.81(4.15)	10.64(4.28)*
Mean	12.19(3.70)	12.52(3.71)	11.86(3.68)

Asterisks (1, 2 and 3) denote statistically significant sex differences respectively at the 5, 1 and .1 per cent levels determined by t tests.

The correlations between the national competitiveness means, economic growth and per capita incomes are given in *Table 12* and are presented, as with the previous personality traits, for the nations as a whole, first including and then excluding the United Arab Emirates, and for the economically developed and developing nations separately.

It will be seen that there is a substantial and statistically significant correlation of 0.48 between national levels of competitiveness and rates of economic growth among the whole set of nations and that this rises to 0.59 when the United Arab Emirates are excluded. The correlations remain high and statistically significant within the two subgroups of economically developed and economically developing nations. In addition, national levels of competitiveness are significantly negatively correlated at -0.34 with per capita incomes among the nations as a whole (and -0.50 with the United Arab Emirates excluded) and at about the same level among the economically developed and economically developing nations.

Table 12: Correlations between national means for Competitiveness and economic growth and per capita incomes (decimal points omitted)

	All Countries	41 Countries	Developed Countries	Developing Countries
Economic Growth	48**	59***	53**	59**
Per capita Income	−34**	−50***	−31	−32

Asterisks (1, 2 and 3) denote statistical significance at the 5, 1 and .1 per cent levels respectively.

This set of results is the most interesting obtained so far in the study and clearly gives some support to Schumpeter's thesis that a high level of competitiveness is a significant factor in economic growth. The negative correlations between competitiveness and per capita incomes suggest that poverty contributes to competitiveness and that competitiveness declines in societies as they become more affluent.

The sex differences results show that males are significantly higher on competitiveness than females in 20 countries, in line with the results found by Spence and Helmreich in the United States. Curiously Iraq is the one country in which females score higher on competitiveness than males, although there are a further 22 countries in which there are no significant sex differences. The results as a whole suggest that while there is some overall tendency for males to score more highly on competitiveness than females, this is not a cultural universal.

8   Achievement via Conformity

The traits considered hitherto measure different aspects of a person's motivation for achievement as an individual. However, man is a social animal and many people are motivated to achieve as members of a social group and through conforming to group norms and objectives. The classical description of this personality is W H White's *The Organisation Man*, the person who identifies with the working group's objectives and makes them his own.[42] The organisation man wears the appropriate clothes, drives the appropriate car, holds the appropriate opinions and has the appropriate wife. But while it is possible to deride this degree of conformity, it expresses a personal identification with the organisation which almost certainly contributes to the organisation's success. In a national economy both individual drives for achievement and drives for achievement via conformity make a useful contribution. Individualistic motives drive the entrepreneur and the inventor, while achievement via conformity motives are important in large firms which need a sense of common purpose and commitment to group objectives.

It has often been suggested that achievement via conformity is high in Japan. Many of the large Japanese firms have their own song and uniform; Japanese workers frequently do not take all their vacation entitlement; and the Japanese tend to stay in one firm throughout their working lives to a greater extent than in other countries. These features of the Japanese are suggestive of a high level of achievement via conformity and may have contributed to the outstanding Japanese commercial successes in the post World War Two decades.

In the study the trait is measured by Gough's Achievement via Conformity Scale. The first question runs 'I liked school', a simple question identifying those who conformed to the group norms and

Table 13: Means and standard deviations for the Achievement via Conformity Scale

Country	Total	Males	Females
Argentina	23.91(2.64)	24.02(2.77)	23.79(2.56)
Australia	24.03(3.17)	23.83(3.33)	24.23(3.01)
Bangladesh	–	–	–
Belgium	23.60(2.82)	23.92(2.80)	23.81(2.83)
Brazil	25.41(2.60)	25.70(2.54)	25.11(2.66)*
Bulgaria	22.00(2.81)	21.90(2.67)	22.09(2.94)
Canada	24.63(2.95)	24.14(3.16)	25.12(2.81)*
Chile	23.25(3.06)	23.20(3.19)	23.30(2.93)
China	23.26(2.47)	23.18(2.66)	23.33(2.28)
Colombia	24.48(2.94)	24.74(2.68)	24.22(3.17)
Egypt	23.69(3.26)	23.69(4.01)	23.68(2.51)
France	22.89(3.63)	22.56(3.29)	23.21(3.97)*
Germany	21.32(3.02)	21.70(2.99)	20.94(3.05)*
Greece	23.82(2.82)	24.06(2.83)	23.58(2.81)
Hong Kong	22.05(2.82)	22.07(2.81)	22.03(2.83)
Iceland	24.16(2.74)	24.31(2.92)	24.01(2.56)
India	23.40(3.37)	22.57(3.53)	24.22(3.20)***
Iraq	21.31(4.24)	21.33(4.40)	21.29(4.07)
Ireland	22.95(3.47)	22.59(3.62)	23.30(3.31)
Israel	23.76(2.78)	24.12(2.50)	23.39(3.06)
Japan	21.84(3.24)	21.42(3.63)	22.26(2.85)*
Jordan	22.76(2.72)	22.77(2.87)	22.75(2.56)
Korea	23.79(2.82)	24.06(2.81)	23.51(2.83)
Mexico	25.64(2.63)	25.68(2.62)	25.60(2.63)
New Zealand	23.67(3.25)	23.47(3.42)	23.86(3.08)
Norway	23.54(2.78)	23.43(2.64)	23.65(2.92)
Poland	22.48(3.21)	22.57(3.36)	22.38(3.05)
Portugal	22.77(2.65)	22.84(2.44)	22.70(2.86)
Romania	21.57(2.83)	21.66(2.93)	21.48(2.77)
Singapore	24.52(2.43)	24.60(2.52)	24.44(2.39)
South Africa	20.93(2.83)	20.68(2.98)	21.17(2.80)*
Spain	22.83(3.01)	22.84(3.01)	22.81(3.01)
Sweden	23.56(2.75)	23.53(2.62)	23.59(2.88)
Switzerland	23.05(2.93)	22.97(2.97)	23.13(2.88)
Syria	22.06(2.37)	21.83(2.52)	22.29(2.20)
Taiwan	23.62(2.93)	23.71(2.98)	23.52(2.88)
Transkei	23.96(2.59)	23.92(2.51)	23.99(2.66)
Turkey	23.30(2.77)	22.93(2.87)	23.67(2.66)*
UAE	23.39(2.56)	23.61(2.58)	23.17(2.53)
UK	23.63(3.35)	23.30(3.42)	23.96(3.27)*
USA	24.61(2.98)	24.22(3.18)	24.99(2.78)***
Venezuela	25.68(2.99)	25.43(2.79)	25.92(3.19)
Yugoslavia	23.22(2.46)	22.43(2.97)	23.10(2.61)*
Mean	23.34(2.94)	23.26(2.98)	23.39(2.88)

Asterisks (1, 2 and 3) denote statistically significant sex differences respectively at the 5, 1 and .1 per cent levels determined by t tests.

expectations which society demands of school children. The questionnaire consists of 10 questions answered yes (3), not sure (2) or no (1), thus yielding a possible maximum of 30.

The results of the study for the Achievement via Conformity Scale are set out in *Table 13*, which gives the means for the nations weighting the sexes equally followed by the means for males and females separately. The correlation between the means for males and females across countries is 0.90. This is highly statistically significant and indicates a good reliability of the scale as assessed by the consistency between the sexes across the nations.

The correlations between the national achievement via conformity means and economic growth and per capita incomes are shown in *Table 14*. It will be seen that there are no statistically significant correlations between achievement via conformity means and rates of economic growth or per capita incomes in either the total samples or among the economically developed or the economically developing countries considered separately.

Table 14: Correlations between the Achievement via Conformity Scale, economic growth rates and per capita income (decimal points omitted)

	All Countries	41 Countries	Developed Countries	Developing Countries
Economic Growth	−03	−06	04	−11
Per capita Income	11	12	17	07

Examination of the sex difference in achievement via conformity shows that females obtain significantly higher scores in 8 countries, namely Canada, France, India, South Africa, Turkey, the UK, the USA, and Yugoslavia while males obtain significantly higher scores in Brazil and Germany. However, considering the nations as a whole there is little overall difference between the sexes on this trait.

9 Valuation of Money

In all countries money is used as a motivator for work effort. In organisations there are hierarchies of grades which carry differential salaries the object of which is to motivate people to work efficiently to obtain promotion to higher grades. Frequently there are in addition incentive payments of various kinds for efficient work. In small businesses, shops, farms and so on the annual profits are the incentive for the owners to work efficiently.

Money is not of course the only motive for working. A number of sociologists and psychologists belonging to the human relations in industry movement have played down the importance of money as a motivator and stressed job satisfaction and other non-financial considerations. There is nevertheless little doubt that money remains a powerful motivation for work effort for many people. Numerous studies have shown that people respond with greater work effort when they are offered financial incentives.[43] It is probable, however, that people differ in the importance they attach to money and therefore in the degree to which they will work hard in order to obtain it and it may be that there are national differences in the strength of the value attached to money. In the study the valuation of money was measured by a short version of a scale constructed by Furnham.[44] The full scale consists of 18 questions but this was considered too long for inclusion in the study. The five questions with the highest loadings (correlations) with the factor were therefore selected for use in the study. The first question runs 'I firmly believe that money can solve all my problems'. The questions are answered on a 7 point scale from 6 (very much) to 0 (not at all), thus yielding a possible maximum score of 30.

Furnham found in his work in Britain that males had higher average scores than females on valuation of money and that working class people had higher scores than middle class. High valuation of

Table 15: Means and standard deviations for the Valuation of Money Scale

Country	Total	Males	Females
Argentina	7.85(4.97)	9.42(5.31)	6.28(4.63)***
Australia	7.12(5.91)	7.50(5.96)	6.47(5.85)
Bangladesh	14.60(6.30)	15.81(6.94)	13.38(5.66)***
Belgium	7.11(6.07)	8.17(6.64)	6.66(5.23)**
Brazil	13.16(5.99)	13.63(6.03)	12.68(5.95)
Bulgaria	11.09(7.38)	13.49(7.48)	8.68(7.27)***
Canada	9.07(6.67)	9.71(7.17)	8.42(6.16)
Chile	11.78(5.98)	12.07(6.24)	11.48(5.71)
China	11.76(6.27)	13.52(6.39)	9.99(6.14)***
Colombia	12.64(5.79)	13.57(5.66)	11.71(5.79)**
Egypt	11.18(6.57)	13.15(6.66)	9.21(6.48)***
France	9.12(6.34)	10.35(7.11)	7.88(5.57)***
Germany	5.70(5.17)	6.61(5.61)	4.78(4.73)**
Greece	13.75(5.62)	14.50(7.31)	12.99(3.93)*
Hong Kong	13.45(5.66)	14.28(5.75)	12.70(5.56)*
Iceland	7.53(6.27)	9.70(7.27)	5.35(5.27)***
India	12.52(7.30)	12.38(7.66)	12.65(6.94)
Iraq	13.77(5.88)	15.39(5.77)	12.14(5.99)***
Ireland	7.84(6.05)	9.05(6.46)	6.62(5.64)***
Israel	10.37(6.45)	12.45(7.08)	8.29(5.82)***
Japan	11.01(5.22)	11.90(5.59)	10.12(4.85)***
Jordan	12.81(6.98)	14.57(6.93)	11.05(6.59)***
Korea	10.89(6.56)	11.65(6.60)	10.13(6.51)*
Mexico	10.86(6.27)	12.10(6.44)	9.61(6.10)***
New Zealand	8.55(6.21)	9.54(6.71)	7.56(5.71)**
Norway	4.25(4.66)	3.62(4.64)	4.88(4.67)
Poland	7.04(6.05)	8.99(6.72)	5.08(5.37)***
Portugal	10.32(5.24)	11.32(5.95)	9.31(4.53)*
Romania	9.95(5.88)	10.96(5.88)	8.94(5.84)*
Singapore	8.51(6.32)	9.03(5.91)	7.98(6.72)
South Africa	12.90(5.62)	14.29(6.18)	11.51(5.05)***
Spain	9.24(5.65)	10.43(6.18)	8.04(5.12)***
Sweden	4.14(4.19)	4.35(4.30)	3.92(4.08)
Switzerland	–	–	–
Syria	13.01(5.98)	14.09(5.62)	11.91(6.15)***
Taiwan	14.50(6.07)	16.17(6.50)	12.83(5.63)***
Transkei	15.32(7.34)	14.35(7.44)	16.28(7.23)*
Turkey	11.20(6.35)	11.45(7.00)	10.94(5.70)
UAE	10.66(6.72)	11.43(6.73)	9.89(6.70)
UK	6.11(5.77)	7.10(6.46)	5.11(5.07)***
USA	10.69(6.55)	12.24(6.84)	9.13(6.26)***
Venezuela	10.39(6.06)	10.39(5.59)	10.38(6.53)
Yugoslavia	10.70(6.85)	12.61(6.89)	8.78(6.81)***
Mean	10.34(6.06)	11.37(6.37)	9.33(5.75)

Asterisks (1, 2 and 3) denote statistically significant sex differences respectively at the 5, 1 and .1 per cent levels determined by t tests.

money scores were also positively associated with a measure of the work ethic.

The results of the study for the Valuation of Money Scale are given in *Table 15*, which shows first the means for the nations weighting the sexes equally followed by the means for males and females separately. The correlation between the means for males and females across countries is 0.87. This is highly statistically significant and indicates a high level of consistency between the scores of the two sexes across the nations.

The correlations between the Valuation of Money Scale and economic growth and per capita incomes are shown in *Table 16*. As with the previous motivational traits, the correlations are given for the whole sample of nations, the whole sample omitting the United Arab Emirates, and for the economically developed and developing nations as separate groups. It will be seen that there are positive correlations between the Valuation of Money Scale and economic growth rates in all four samples, although the correlation of 0.26 among the economically developing nations does not reach statistical significance. The pattern of correlations suggests that the degree to which people value money may be a determinant of economic growth rates at all levels of economic development. This is essentially the thesis proposed by Wiener for the low economic growth of Britain during the present century and the findings lend some support to this theory.

Table 16: Correlations between national means for the Valuation of Money and economic growth and per capita incomes (decimal points omitted)

	All Countries	41 Countries	Developed Countries	Developing Countries
Economic Growth	26*	46***	56**	26
Per capita Income	−52***	−61***	−45*	−40*

Asterisks (1, 2 and 3) denote statistical significance at the 5, 1 and .1 per cent levels respectively.

There are also statistically significant negative associations between the valuation of money and per capita income among all four samples of nations. The result suggests that as people become more affluent they attach less value to money, as might be expected.

The sex differences show a general trend for males to attach more value to money than females. The male scores are higher than females in 40 of the nations, and only in India, Norway and Transkei is this tendency reversed. Probably the reason for this sex difference is that males generally tend to be more competitive than females and money is valued partly as a symbol of competitive success. There are high correlations between the valuation of money and competitiveness across nations, where the correlation is 0.72, and among individuals within nations, as is shown in Chapter 14.

10 Attitudes to Saving

A further dimension to the valuation of money is attitudes towards saving, that is the degree to which people believe in saving and do save to provide a form of security against future misfortunes. The questionnaire used was Yamauchi and Templer's savings scale[45] for which a typical question runs 'I put money aside on a regular basis for the future'. The questions are answered on a 5 point scale from 'strongly agree' (scored 4) to 'strongly disagree' (scored 0). There are 7 items in the scale and a maximum score of 28.

The results of the Attitudes to Savings Scale are given in *Table 17* for the total sample with the sexes weighted equally and for males and females separately. The male-female correlation across countries is +0.88 indicating a highly reliable scale as assessed by the consistency of the male and female means.

The correlations between the Attitudes to Savings Scale means and economic growth rates are shown in *Table 18*. It will be seen that the savings scale is not associated with rates of economic growth among the total sample, but does have a significant correlation of +0.48 among the economically developed nations.

The Attitudes to Savings Scale shows statistically significant negative correlations of −0.40 and −0.41 with per capita incomes for the total sample of nations and the 41 nation sample, showing that people in more affluent nations attach less value to savings. This is possibly a reflection of a similar tendency of people in more affluent countries to attach less value to money noted in the last chapter.

The sex differences in the Savings Scale show a general tendency for males to attach greater value to savings than females. The higher means of males are statistically significant in 13 countries, namely Argentina, Bulgaria, Brazil, China, Egypt, Iraq, Ireland, Poland, Romania, South Africa, Spain, Taiwan and the United

Table 17: Means and standard deviations for the
Attitude to Saving Scale

Country	Total	Males	Females
Argentina	22.67(8.69)	24.78(8.97)	20.56(8.41)***
Australia	18.39(9.27)	18.29(9.51)	18.48(9.03)
Bangladesh	21.73(7.49)	20.56(7.84)	22.89(7.13)**
Belgium	18.57(8.92)	18.51(8.96)	18.63(8.91)
Brazil	27.68(8.26)	28.62(7.51)	26.74(9.01)*
Bulgaria	21.60(9.73)	24.78(8.99)	18.42(10.47)***
Canada	19.04(9.65)	17.75(9.53)	20.32(9.77)
Chile	20.02(9.17)	22.13(8.96)	19.90(9.38)
China	14.87(7.82)	16.12(7.77)	13.61(7.87)**
Colombia	25.18(9.53)	25.37(9.04)	24.99(10.03)
Egypt	18.20(9.25)	20.43(9.22)	15.97(9.27)***
France	17.48(9.34)	17.67(9.90)	17.29(8.78)
Germany	18.86(9.38)	18.78(10.25)	18.94(8.94)
Greece	22.10(9.01)	22.78(9.25)	21.43(8.77)
Hong Kong	20.22(7.56)	20.42(8.14)	20.01(6.97)
Iceland	17.49(8.65)	18.36(8.46)	16.62(8.83)
India	24.37(8.86)	24.80(8.90)	23.93(8.82)
Iraq	21.62(9.22)	22.52(9.46)	20.71(8.98)*
Ireland	13.34(8.90)	*l49⊏*14.90(9.41)	11.75(8.39)**
Israel	22.81(8.17)	22.15(8.70)	23.47(7.64)
Japan	13.18(7.63)	12.48(7.63)	13.87(7.63)
Jordan	20.35(7.99)	21.17(8.07)	19.54(7.86)
Korea	20.54(9.19)	20.34(8.58)	20.74(9.79)
Mexico	24.43(10.13)	25.02(10.01)	23.83(10.25)
New Zealand	17.75(8.51)	18.15(8.54)	17.34(8.48)
Norway	15.50(7.57)	15.46(7.20)	15.54(7.93)
Poland	18.10(9.25)	20.25(9.47)	15.94(9.02)***
Portugal	25.56(7.44)	26.10(7.43)	25.03(7.44)
Romania	15.10(8.68)	16.50(8.96)	13.71(8.40)*
Singapore	22.31(9.40)	22.26(9.05)	22.35(9.75)
South Africa	23.09(7.63)	23.65(7.46)	22.53(7.80)*
Spain	16.59(8.29)	17.60(8.47)	15.57(8.08)*
Sweden	10.89(6.55)	10.60(6.41)	11.15(6.68)
Switzerland	13.92(8.74)	14.58(9.92)	13.25(7.56)
Syria	21.38(6.68)	22.10(6.21)	20.64(7.06)
Taiwan	24.15(9.43)	26.12(9.55)	22.17(9.30)***
Transkei	27.62(8.48)	26.04(9.26)	29.20(7.70)***
Turkey	18.03(9.00)	18.35(9.97)	17.71(8.03)
UAE	17.71(8.96)	19.93(9.16)	15.43(8.36)***
UK	15.97(8.90)	16.25(9.37)	15.68(8.43)
USA	22.41(8.92)	22.82(9.01)	22.09(8.83)
Venezuela	17.29(7.74)	16.71(7.81)	17.86(7.66)
Yugoslavia	16.54(9.03)	16.88(9.89)	16.19(8.16)
Mean	19.41(8.63)	20.31(8.75)	19.22(8.50)

Asterisks (1, 2 and 3) denote statistically significant sex differences respectively
at the 5, 1 and .1 per cent levels determined by t tests.

Table 18: Correlations between the Attitudes to Saving means and economic growth and per capita incomes (decimal points omitted)

	All Countries	41 Countries	Developed Countries	Developing Countries
Economic Growth	07	22	48*	−19
Per capita Income	−40**	−41**	−18	06

Asterisks (1 and 2) denote statistical significance at the 5 and 1 per cent levels respectively.

Arab Emirates, and there is a significant tendency for males to obtain higher scores in a further 17 countries. Only in Bangladesh do females attach greater value to savings than males.

11 Occupational Preferences

It was proposed by Wiener that the strength of occupational preferences in different countries can affect economic growth.[46] If careers in the professions and on the land are favoured more than those in business, the business sector of society will be to some degree deprived of talent and demoralised, business enterprise will suffer and national economic growth rates reduced.

In order to test this theory the questionnaire included the question 'How much would you like to do each of these jobs?' The jobs to be evaluated were doctor, social worker, director of large public company ('organisation' was substituted in socialist countries), teacher, country landowner and farmer, and owner of small business. It was considered that this would give a good spread of occupations in the professions, land and business. The responses were given on a 7 point scale and scored 6 (very much) to 0 (not at all) and each occupation was scored separately. The occupational preferences scales were first examined for male-female correlations across the countries. These are 0.82 (doctor), 0.80 (social worker), 0.82 (company director), 0.81 (teacher), 0.85 (country landowner and farmer) and 0.80 (owner of small business). All the correlations are high and indicate good reliability of the scales as assessed by the consistency of male and female means.

The means for the nations for the six occupational preferences are set out in *Tables 19* through *24*. The first figures are the means for the total sample, with males and females weighted equally, and these are followed by the means for males and females separately.

The correlations between the occupational preference means and economic growth rates and per capita incomes are given in *Table 25*. It will be seen that there are no statistically significant correlations between any of the occupational preferences and economic growth rates or per capita incomes among the total sample

Table 19: Means and standard deviations for evaluations of the occupation of doctor

Country	Total	Males	Females
Argentina	3.00(2.12)	3.43(2.16)	2.57(2.07)***
Australia	2.77(2.00)	2.83(1.88)	2.71(2.12)
Bangladesh	2.96(2.16)	2.41(2.03)	3.51(2.28)***
Belgium	3.02(2.06)	3.09(2.11)	2.94(2.02)
Brazil	2.08(2.00)	2.17(1.98)	1.99(2.02)
Bulgaria	3.70(2.06)	3.48(2.09)	3.92(2.02)
Canada	2.80(2.07)	2.65(2.05)	2.95(2.08)
Chile	5.14(1.16)	4.88(1.41)	5.31(0.91)**
China	2.94(1.87)	3.05(1.77)	2.84(1.96)
Colombia	3.42(2.13)	3.29(2.11)	3.55(2.15)
Egypt	2.67(2.51)	2.66(2.36)	2.68(2.66)
France	2.98(2.04)	2.72(1.98)	3.00(2.09)
Germany	2.87(2.12)	3.01(2.14)	2.78(2.09)
Greece	1.87(2.00)	1.43(1.87)	2.30(2.13)***
Hong Kong	2.40(1.98)	2.71(2.03)	2.08(1.92)*
Iceland	2.40(2.10)	2.50(2.14)	2.29(2.06)
India	3.63(1.95)	3.38(1.81)	3.87(2.08)*
Iraq	2.18(2.21)	2.39(2.19)	1.97(2.23)*
Ireland	2.10(2.05)	2.01(2.05)	2.15(2.06)
Israel	4.01(1.80)	4.01(1.80)	4.01(1.80)
Japan	3.36(1.64)	3.18(1.68)	3.53(1.59)*
Jordan	2.29(2.14)	2.17(2.06)	2.40(2.22)
Korea	1.86(1.95)	1.78(1.89)	1.97(2.01)
Mexico	3.83(2.04)	3.76(2.01)	3.90(2.07)
New Zealand	2.74(1.97)	2.62(1.99)	2.86(1.95)
Norway	4.15(1.70)	3.95(1.90)	4.35(1.50)
Poland	2.11(2.05)	2.09(2.00)	2.13(2.09)
Portugal	2.52(1.80)	2.68(1.74)	2.35(1.85)
Romania	3.51(1.60)	3.74(1.55)	3.28(1.64)*
Singapore	3.05(2.31)	3.04(2.24)	3.05(2.38)
South Africa	3.02(1.79)	3.11(1.84)	2.92(1.74)
Spain	3.40(2.40)	3.33(2.02)	3.47(2.05)
Sweden	3.26(1.99)	3.45(1.85)	3.06(2.13)
Switzerland	3.33(1.74)	3.29(1.75)	3.37(1.73)
Syria	2.39(2.02)	2.50(2.04)	2.28(2.01)
Taiwan	2.54(2.09)	2.73(2.15)	2.34(2.02)
Transkei	2.55(2.17)	2.70(2.06)	2.40(2.27)
Turkey	1.93(1.93)	1.69(1.85)	2.16(2.00)*
UAE	2.40(2.20)	2.12(2.09)	2.67(2.31)*
UK	2.12(2.00)	2.13(2.00)	2.11(2.00)
USA	2.50(1.90)	2.69(1.87)	2.31(1.92)*
Venezuela	2.60(2.36)	2.77(2.28)	3.43(2.44)*
Yugoslavia	3.11(2.15)	2.65(2.19)	3.56(2.11)***
Mean	2.87(2.02)	2.82(2.01)	2.89(2.03)

Asterisks (1, 2 and 3) denote statistically significant sex differences respectively at the 5, 1 and .1 per cent levels determined by t tests.

75

Table 20: Means and standard deviations for evaluations of the occupation of social worker

Country	Total	Males	Females
Argentina	2.74(1.99)	2.00(1.90)	3.48(2.07)***
Australia	3.33(1.99)	3.18(1.96)	3.48(2.01)
Bangladesh	3.35(1.87)	3.51(1.90)	3.19(1.84)
Belgium	2.40(2.09)	2.19(2.10)	2.61(2.06)
Brazil	2.19(1.82)	1.85(1.69)	2.53(1.94)***
Bulgaria	–	–	–
Canada	2.67(1.72)	1.80(1.65)	3.54(1.79)***
Chile	4.57(1.46)	4.27(1.64)	4.86(1.28)**
China	2.71(1.80)	2.69(1.78)	2.72(1.81)
Colombia	2.94(1.90)	2.47(1.90)	3.40(1.80)***
Egypt	2.62(2.28)	2.12(2.14)	3.12(2.42)***
France	2.28(2.00)	1.96(1.94)	2.60(2.06)**
Germany	3.19(1.96)	2.98(1.98)	3.40(1.93)
Greece	2.70(1.99)	1.88(1.96)	3.52(2.02)***
Hong Kong	2.29(1.80)	2.16(1.83)	2.41(1.76)
Iceland	1.66(1.76)	1.27(1.62)	2.04(1.90)***
India	4.12(1.91)	4.01(2.07)	4.23(1.74)
Iraq	2.53(2.16)	2.40(2.04)	2.65(2.28)
Ireland	2.43(2.03)	2.07(1.84)	2.75(2.15)**
Israel	2.48(1.77)	–	–
Japan	3.17(1.50)	2.95(1.59)	3.38(1.41)**
Jordan	3.24(2.05)	3.07(2.03)	3.42(2.06)
Korea	3.63(1.80)	3.59(1.66)	3.67(1.93)
Mexico	2.89(1.84)	2.70(1.79)	3.07(1.89)*
New Zealand	2.34(1.80)	1.82(1.73)	2.85(1.86)***
Norway	4.32(1.50)	4.22(1.50)	4.41(1.50)
Poland	0.88(1.33)	0.94(1.37)	0.81(1.28)
Portugal	3.02(1.68)	2.77(1.63)	3.26(1.72)
Romania	2.36(1.61)	2.30(1.68)	2.42(1.54)
Singapore	3.36(1.83)	3.19(1.83)	3.53(1.82)
South Africa	3.23(1.65)	2.85(1.61)	3.60(1.69)***
Spain	2.12(1.83)	1.72(1.73)	2.52(1.92)***
Sweden	2.31(1.71)	2.20(1.57)	2.41(1.85)
Switzerland	3.80(1.70)	3.37(1.73)	4.23(1.66)***
Syria	2.86(1.91)	2.77(1.85)	2.94(1.97)
Taiwan	3.28(1.64)	3.06(1.72)	3.52(1.56)*
Transkei	3.56(2.07)	3.28(2.06)	3.84(2.08)*
Turkey	2.80(1.97)	2.59(1.93)	3.00(2.00)
UAE	2.95(2.17)	2.61(2.06)	3.28(2.27)*
UK	2.13(1.93)	1.70(1.87)	2.55(1.98)***
USA	2.87(1.74)	2.47(1.64)	3.26(1.84)***
Venezuela	3.13(2.29)	2.85(2.21)	3.40(2.37)*
Yugoslavia	3.16(2.05)	2.27(2.18)	4.05(1.92)***
Mean	2.87(1.85)	2.59(1.83)	3.17(1.86)

Asterisks (1, 2 and 3) denote statistically significant sex differences respectively at the 5, 1 and .1 per cent levels determined by t tests.

Table 21: Means and standard deviations for evaluations of the occupation of company director

Country	Total	Males	Females
Argentina	1.64(1.82)	1.70(1.84)	1.57(1.79)
Australia	3.28(2.17)	3.28(2.12)	3.28(2.21)
Bangladesh	3.32(1.83)	3.62(1.86)	3.02(1.80)*
Belgium	2.48(2.13)	3.05(2.11)	1.91(1.99)***
Brazil	3.21(1.98)	3.33(1.86)	3.08(2.10)
Bulgaria	1.93(1.90)	2.31(2.01)	1.54(1.78)***
Canada	3.18(2.13)	3.61(2.10)	2.74(2.15)*
Chile	4.31(1.55)	4.18(1.77)	4.44(1.33)
China	3.73(1.84)	4.19(1.78)	3.27(1.92)***
Colombia	3.45(2.04)	3.56(1.95)	3.33(2.12)
Egypt	3.14(2.22)	3.89(2.09)	2.38(2.34)***
France	2.53(2.15)	2.67(2.23)	2.38(2.07)
Germany	1.62(1.79)	1.83(1.86)	1.40(1.71)*
Greece	3.55(2.10)	3.69(2.07)	3.41(2.12)
Hong Kong	3.94(1.71)	4.10(1.76)	3.78(1.66)
Iceland	3.33(1.93)	3.62(1.86)	3.04(2.07)***
India	3.69(2.21)	3.67(2.29)	3.71(2.12)
Iraq	2.93(2.17)	3.08(2.11)	2.78(2.22)
Ireland	3.57(2.15)	3.77(2.08)	3.37(2.21)
Israel	4.32(1.74)	–	–
Japan	2.93(1.63)	2.80(1.73)	3.05(1.53)
Jordan	3.04(2.20)	3.66(2.11)	2.44(2.14)***
Korea	3.36(1.93)	3.66(1.82)	3.05(2.04)**
Mexico	3.58(2.08)	3.95(1.89)	3.20(2.27)***
New Zealand	3.27(2.01)	3.35(1.97)	3.18(2.04)
Norway	2.44(1.95)	2.32(2.00)	2.55(1.90)
Poland	1.83(1.85)	2.53(2.12)	1.13(1.57)***
Portugal	2.86(1.74)	3.00(1.73)	2.72(1.75)
Romania	2.61(1.77)	2.64(1.79)	2.58(1.75)
Singapore	2.97(1.98)	3.27(1.80)	2.66(2.15)**
South Africa	4.23(1.77)	4.42(1.76)	4.04(1.78)**
Spain	3.07(2.19)	3.36(2.14)	2.77(2.23)**
Sweden	2.20(2.01)	2.39(1.99)	2.00(2.02)
Switzerland	2.18(1.94)	2.53(2.02)	1.82(1.85)**
Syria	2.81(2.10)	3.27(1.99)	2.34(2.11)***
Taiwan	3.67(1.70)	4.01(1.68)	3.32(1.71)***
Transkei	2.82(2.13)	3.31(2.08)	2.33(2.17)***
Turkey	4.61(1.72)	4.34(1.85)	4.87(1.58)**
UAE	3.24(2.30)	3.69(2.15)	2.79(2.45)**
UK	3.01(2.19)	3.23(2.25)	2.78(2.12)*
USA	3.35(1.90)	3.74(1.87)	2.96(1.92)***
Venezuela	3.41(2.41)	3.51(2.20)	3.31(2.62)
Yugoslavia	2.64(2.08)	2.93(2.14)	2.34(2.01)**
Mean	3.10(1.96)	3.31(1.93)	2.83(1.99)

Asterisks (1, 2 and 3) denote statistically significant sex differences respectively at the 5, 1 and .1 per cent levels determined by t tests.

Table 22: Means and standard deviations for evaluations of the occupation of teacher

Country	Total	Males	Females
Argentina	2.54(2.01)	2.15(1.87)	2.93(2.15)***
Australia	3.64(1.93)	3.60(1.91)	3.67(1.94)
Bangladesh	4.07(1.83)	3.38(2.01)	4.76(1.65)***
Belgium	3.80(1.90)	3.79(1.90)	3.81(1.91)
Brazil	2.66(1.94)	2.68(1.85)	2.64(2.03)
Bulgaria	1.82(1.97)	1.84(1.96)	1.79(1.98)
Canada	3.93(1.80)	3.41(1.88)	4.44(1.72)***
Chile	5.04(1.31)	4.87(1.40)	5.21(1.22)
China	2.26(1.80)	2.04(1.73)	2.49(1.84)*
Colombia	3.22(2.15)	3.04(2.05)	3.39(2.24)
Egypt	2.78(2.41)	2.89(2.32)	2.66(2.49)
France	3.42(2.08)	3.47(2.12)	3.36(2.04)
Germany	3.13(2.07)	3.58(2.02)	2.68(2.12)***
Greece	2.97(2.03)	2.39(1.99)	3.55(2.06)***
Hong Kong	2.32(1.85)	2.33(1.85)	2.30(1.85)
Iceland	2.87(1.84)	2.68(1.75)	3.05(1.93)
India	3.96(1.98)	4.01(1.86)	3.90(2.10)
Iraq	2.90(2.27)	3.12(2.13)	2.67(2.40)*
Ireland	2.92(1.91)	2.78(1.87)	3.03(2.08)
Israel	3.09(1.64)	–	–
Japan	3.42(1.84)	3.40(1.92)	3.43(1.76)
Jordan	3.10(2.40)	2.62(2.32)	3.59(2.38)***
Korea	3.49(1.94)	3.49(1.79)	3.49(2.08)
Mexico	3.48(1.91)	3.62(1.87)	3.33(1.95)
New Zealand	2.93(1.94)	2.93(1.80)	2.93(2.07)
Norway	3.41(1.75)	3.35(1.80)	3.47(1.70)
Poland	4.03(1.63)	3.81(1.88)	4.28(1.38)
Portugal	4.43(1.65)	4.26(1.71)	4.61(1.58)
Romania	3.45(1.61)	2.98(1.55)	3.91(1.67)***
Singapore	3.50(1.98)	3.48(1.81)	3.52(2.14)
South Africa	3.05(1.73)	2.97(1.73)	3.13(1.72)
Spain	2.53(1.90)	2.46(1.86)	2.59(1.93)
Sweden	3.12(1.90)	3.27(1.82)	2.97(1.97)
Switzerland	3.91(1.66)	3.94(1.58)	3.88(1.74)
Syria	3.00(2.15)	2.79(2.18)	3.21(2.11)
Taiwan	3.25(1.77)	3.11(1.79)	3.38(1.75)
Transkei	5.23(1.47)	5.24(1.34)	5.21(1.60)
Turkey	2.54(1.92)	2.59(1.97)	2.48(1.86)
UAE	2.86(2.39)	2.76(2.32)	2.96(2.45)
UK	2.68(2.00)	2.48(2.00)	2.88(2.00)*
USA	4.26(1.86)	4.17(1.74)	4.34(1.93)
Venezuela	3.26(2.35)	3.23(2.19)	3.28(2.58)
Yugoslavia	3.33(2.01)	2.85(2.08)	3.81(1.94)***
Mean	3.29(1.92)	3.19(1.89)	3.41(1.95)

Asterisks (1, 2 and 3) denote statistically significant sex differences respectively at the 5, 1 and .1 per cent levels determined by t tests.

Table 23: Means and standard deviations for evaluations of the occupation of country landowner and farmer

Country	Total	Males	Females
Argentina	3.61(1.99)	4.59(1.87)	2.64(2.13)***
Australia	2.19(1.85)	2.46(1.87)	1.92(1.83)
Bangladesh	1.58(1.79)	1.90(1.70)	1.25(1.78)**
Belgium	2.07(1.97)	2.28(1.97)	1.87(1.95)
Brazil	3.91(1.97)	3.93(1.91)	3.88(2.03)
Bulgaria	0.88(1.47)	1.04(1.56)	0.72(1.33)
Canada	1.97(1.83)	2.12(1.86)	1.81(1.92)
Chile	3.99(1.57)	3.85(1.70)	4.12(1.44)
China	1.16(1.44)	1.37(1.48)	0.95(1.43)*
Colombia	3.20(1.97)	3.38(1.87)	3.02(2.05)
Egypt	2.31(2.37)	2.61(2.28)	2.01(2.45)*
France	1.34(1.80)	1.62(1.93)	1.05(1.67)***
Germany	2.29(1.93)	2.28(1.82)	2.29(2.04)
Greece	1.75(1.89)	2.10(1.96)	1.40(1.71)***
Hong Kong	1.86(1.82)	2.25(1.94)	1.46(1.69)***
Iceland	2.02(1.97)	2.11(1.97)	1.92(1.97)
India	2.09(1.90)	2.46(2.00)	1.76(1.82)***
Iraq	2.32(2.14)	2.86(2.13)	1.77(2.14)***
Ireland	2.32(2.12)	2.55(2.00)	2.08(2.24)
Israel	3.09(1.64)	–	–
Japan	3.42(1.89)	2.41(1.64)	2.54(1.51)
Jordan	3.10(2.40)	3.70(2.14)	3.20(2.16)*
Korea	3.49(1.94)	1.96(1.73)	1.63(1.78)
Mexico	3.48(1.91)	3.31(1.86)	2.33(1.96)***
New Zealand	2.93(1.94)	2.60(2.05)	2.30(1.99)
Norway	3.41(1.75)	3.30(2.20)	2.64(1.90)
Poland	4.03(1.63)	2.69(2.08)	1.79(2.02)***
Portugal	4.43(1.65)	2.39(1.78)	1.75(1.50)
Romania	3.45(1.61)	1.86(1.51)	1.42(1.34)*
Singapore	3.50(1.98)	2.60(1.91)	2.40(2.07)
South Africa	3.05(1.73)	2.75(1.77)	2.04(1.49)***
Spain	2.53(1.90)	2.18(1.93)	1.57(1.74)**
Sweden	3.12(1.90)	1.71(1.92)	2.04(1.94)
Switzerland	3.91(1.66)	2.19(1.88) 1·8 3	1.72(1.87)
Syria	3.00(2.15)	3.73(1.86)	2.52(2.30)***
Taiwan	3.25(1.77)	2.33(1.84)	1.98(1.70)
Transkei	5.23(1.47)	2.75(1.98)	2.23(2.19)*
Turkey	2.54(1.92)	2.12(1.91)	1.64(1.73)*
UAE	2.86(2.39)	3.57(2.26)	2.78(2.37)**
UK	2.68(2.00)	2.75(2.11)	2.14(2.03)***
USA	4.26(1.86)	2.66(1.98)	1.94(2.03)***
Venezuela	3.26(2.35)	3.87(2.15)	3.57(2.51)
Yugoslavia	3.33(2.01)	2.25(2.05)	2.26(1.94)
Mean	2.38(1.91)	2.60(1.91)	2.10(1.90)

Asterisks (1, 2 and 3) denote statistically significant sex differences respectively at the 5, 1 and .1 per cent levels determined by t tests.

Table 24: Means and standard deviations for evaluations of the occupation of small business owner

Country	Total	Males	Females
Argentina	2.03(1.72)	2.14(1.75)	1.91(1.68)
Australia	3.23(1.87)	3.05(1.87)	3.41(1.86)
Bangladesh	2.49(2.00)	3.08(2.17)	1.98(1.82)***
Belgium	3.14(2.02)	3.54(1.90)	2.73(2.06)***
Brazil	3.09(1.74)	3.95(1.71)	3.85(1.76)
Bulgaria	2.34(2.02)	2.87(2.09)	1.81(1.95)***
Canada	3.98(1.68)	4.33(1.41)	3.62(1.95)*
Chile	3.51(1.64)	3.42(1.75)	3.60(1.53)
China	1.25(1.53)	1.47(1.60)	1.02(1.46)**
Colombia	3.95(2.01)	4.17(1.78)	3.73(2.21)
Egypt	3.90(2.16)	4.12(2.10)	3.67(2.21)
France	2.71(2.18)	2.92(2.20)	2.49(2.14)
Germany	2.65(1.89)	2.96(1.81)	2.33(1.96)**
Greece	3.26(1.96)	3.53(1.89)	2.99(2.02)*
Hong Kong	3.92(1.62)	3.96(1.62)	3.87(1.62)
Iceland	4.22(1.83)	4.47(1.64)	3.97(2.01)*
India	2.98(2.32)	3.05(2.23)	2.91(2.41)
Iraq	2.90(2.08)	3.16(1.94)	2.63(2.22)**
Ireland	3.98(1.92)	4.05(1.76)	3.90(2.08)
Israel	3.06(1.65)	–	–
Japan	3.27(1.61)	3.49(1.67)	3.04(1.55)**
Jordan	3.37(2.04)	3.53(1.93)	3.21(2.14)
Korea	3.29(1.95)	3.73(1.88)	2.85(2.02)***
Mexico	3.74(1.96)	4.11(1.82)	3.37(1.80)***
New Zealand	3.50(1.79)	3.64(1.72)	3.36(1.85)
Norway	3.47(1.85)	3.60(1.90)	3.33(1.80)
Poland	3.39(2.02)	4.26(1.90)	2.51(2.13)***
Portugal	3.00(1.57)	3.39(1.45)	2.61(1.68)*
Romania	2.67(1.63)	3.09(1.70)	2.24(1.55)***
Singapore	2.99(1.93)	3.15(1.76)	2.82(2.10)
South Africa	4.30(1.72)	4.32(1.71)	4.27(1.72)
Spain	3.08(1.97)	3.42(1.91)	2.74(2.02)***
Sweden	3.53(1.94)	3.52(1.83)	3.53(2.04)
Switzerland	2.51(1.88)	2.99(1.95)	2.03(1.81)***
Syria	3.21(1.98)	3.72(1.77)	2.69(2.06)***
Taiwan	3.18(1.75)	3.50(1.82)	2.86(1.68)***
Transkei	3.58(2.11)	3.51(2.06)	3.65(2.15)
Turkey	3.48(1.96)	3.38(2.05)	3.58(1.86)
UAE	3.28(2.21)	3.78(2.10)	2.78(2.32)***
UK	3.87(1.88)	3.90(1.83)	3.84(1.93)
USA	4.29(1.62)	4.43(1.56)	4.14(1.68)*
Venezuela	3.60(2.25)	3.44(2.13)	3.76(2.26)
Yugoslavia	4.23(1.90)	4.59(1.77)	3.86(2.03)***
Mean	3.30(1.98)	3.54(1.84)	3.08(1.93)

Asterisks (1, 2 and 3) denote statistically significant sex differences respectively at the 5, 1 and .1 per cent levels determined by t tests.

of nations. However, on the 41 nation sample there are statistically significant negative correlations between rates of economic growth and valuation of the occupations of doctor (-0.26) and teacher (-0.30), suggesting that a tendency among young people to have a high regard for these occupations may retard economic growth rates because the most talented will tend to make their careers in the caring professions rather than in economically productive occupations.

Among the economically developed nations a similar tendency seems to be present expressed in the significant correlation of $+0.50$ between rates of economic growth and valuation of the occupation of company director. Among the economically developing countries the tendency is again present in the significant negative correlation of -0.43 between economic growth rates and valuation of the occupations of doctor (-0.43) and country landowner and farmer (-0.43), suggesting that high regard for these occupations tends to retard rates of economic growth among this subset of countries. High valuation of the occupation of small business person has no significant association with rates of economic growth in any of the samples of nations.

Wiener's theory that an occupational preference for the life of a country landowner and farmer retards economic growth receives no support among the nations as a whole or among the economically developed nations, where the correlations between the strength of this occupational preference and economic growth rates are 0.06, -0.17 and 0.13. However, there is a statistically significant negative correlation of -0.43 among the economically developing nations, suggesting that among this set of countries a strong wish for agricultural employment acts as a retarding factor on economic growth. It might be expected that among this set of nations there would be a complementary tendency to prefer the business occupations than among the higher growth economies, but there is no tendency for this to be the case.

Turning now to the correlations between the occupational preferences and per capita incomes, it appears in the 41 nation sample that there is a statistically significant negative correlation of -0.27 between per capita income and valuation of the occupation of company director. The same negative associations are present in the economically developed nations, suggesting that as societies become more affluent there is a turning away from the major business occupations. Conversely, in economically developed nations young people have higher valuations of the 'caring professions' of doctor, social worker and teacher, where the correlations with per capita incomes are +0.29, 0.38 and 0.69. The pattern of correlations suggests that as economically developed nations become highly affluent there is a turning away on the part of young people from careers in business towards those in the 'caring professions' of doctor, social worker and teacher.

Let us turn now to the sex differences in occupational preferences. It will be seen that for the career of doctor there is little overall sex difference, although in four countries (Argentina, Hong Kong, Iraq and Romania) the preference for this profession is stronger in males, while in eight countries (Bangladesh, Chile, Greece, Japan, Turkey, United Arab Emirates, Venezuela and Yugoslavia) females have a stronger preference for this profession. For the career of social worker there is a strong trend for females to show greater preference in most countries. The trend is statistically significant in 23 of the countries, namely Argentina, Brazil, Canada, Chile, Colombia, Egypt, France, Greece, Iceland, Ireland, Japan, Mexico, New Zealand, South Africa, Spain, Switzerland, Taiwan, Transkei, United Arab Emirates, UK, USA, Venezuela and Yugoslavia. There are no countries in which males show a stronger preference than females for the profession of social worker.

In the case of the career of company director, males show a stronger preference for this occupation in 22 countries consisting of Bangladesh, Belgium, Bulgaria, Canada, China, Egypt, Germany, Iceland, Korea, Mexico, Poland, Singapore, South Africa, Spain, Switzerland, Syria, Taiwan, Transkei, United Arab Emirates, UK, USA and Yugoslavia. Only in Turkey do females show a stronger preference than males for the career of company director.

For the career of teacher, females tend to have stronger preference in 11 countries, namely Argentina, Bangladesh, Canada, China, Germany, Greece, Jordan, Poland, Romania, UK and Venezuela. The only country where males show a stronger preference for a career in teaching is Iraq.

Table 25: Correlations between occupational preferences and economic growth rates and per capita incomes (decimal points omitted)

	All Countries	41 Countries	Developed Countries	Developing Countries
Doctor				
Economic Growth	–23	–26*	–06	–43*
Per capita Income	00	06	29	–28
Social Worker				
Economic Growth	–01	–05	12	–26
Per capita Income	01	00	38*	–33
Company Director				
Economic Growth	15	23	50**	–02
Per capita Income	–23	–27*	–48*	–36
Teacher				
Economic Growth	–24	–30*	–24	–36
Per capita Income	14	21	69**	–01
Country Landowner				
Economic Growth	06	–17	13	–43*
Per capita Income	–03	–12	16	36
Small Business Owner				
Economic Growth	–03	–06	12	–12
Per capita Income	18	20	17	31

Asterisks (1 and 2) denote statistical significance at the 5 and 1 per cent levels respectively.

With regard to the occupation of country landowner and farmer, males have a stronger preference in 22 countries, namely Argentina, Bangladesh, China, Egypt, France, Greece, Hong Kong, India, Iraq, Jordan, Mexico, Poland, Portugal, Romania, South Africa, Spain, Syria, Transkei, Turkey, United Arab Emirates, UK and USA. There are no countries in which females have a statistically significant stronger preference for the occupation of country landowner and farmer.

The final occupation assessed in the study was owner of small business. Males tended to evaluate this career more highly and the sex difference was significant in 22 countries, namely Bangladesh, Belgium, Bulgaria, Canada, China, Germany, Greece, Iceland, Iraq, Japan, Korea, Mexico, Poland, Portugal, Romania, Spain, Switzerland, Syria, Taiwan, United Arab Emirates, USA and Yugoslavia. There were no countries where females showed a stronger preference than males for the occupation of small business owner.

Considering the sex differences in occupational preferences as a whole, there is an apparent tendency for males to have stronger preferences for those occupations which confer high financial rewards and power, namely director of large company, country landowner and farmer, and owner of small business. Females showed stronger preferences for the caring professions of social worker and teacher. For the occupation of doctor, which generally confers high financial rewards and power but also has a caring dimension, there is no pronounced sex difference, suggesting that the career may tend to appeal to males and females for different reasons. In spite of a few exceptions the sex differences in the perceived desirability of the six occupations show quite striking consistencies among this diverse set of nations.

12 Multiple Regression Analyses of the Contribution of Work Attitudes to Economic Growth

Hitherto the seven psychological traits of the work ethic, achievement motivation, etc and the valuation of the six occupations have been treated as if they were independent variables and their association with rates of economic growth examined on this basis. However, the assumption that the psychological measures are independent is unlikely to be correct. It is probable that the psychological measures have some degree of association with each other and it is also probable that two or more of the psychological factors may combine to affect rates of economic growth.

The method of testing for these possibilities is by the use of multiple regression analysis of the psychological measures on rates of economic growth. Multiple regression analysis serves two purposes. Firstly, it provides 'partial coefficients' of each variable with economic growth rates holding every other variable constant. Secondly, it gives a measure of the contribution of all the psychological measures to rates of economic growth controlling for the associations or 'collinearity' of some of the psychological measures with each other.

It is useful to start by examining the correlation matrix of all the psychological measures with each other and with the economic variables. The matrix is shown in *Table 26*. It will be seen that several of the psychological measures have substantial intercorrelations. For instance, the Work Ethic and Mastery Scales are correlated +0.74 and the Competitiveness and Valuation of Money Scales are also correlated +0.74. These correlations are so high that they suggest a considerable common element in the two pairs of measures.

The multiple regression analyses of the psychological measures

Table 26: Matrix of correlations derived from the 41 nation sample (decimal points omitted)

Measures	1	2	3	4	5	6	7	8	9	10	11	12	13	14
1. Work Ethic														
2. Mastery	76													
3. Competitiveness	04	08												
4. Savings	31	28	40											
5. Achievement Motivation	30	21	21	31										
6. Valuation of Money	-04	10	72	55	17									
7. Achievement via Conformity	58	56	-06	20	19	-09								
8. Doctor	11	10	23	-16	-24	12	-02							
9. Social Worker	01	01	03	17	-17	21	03	49						
10. Company Director	01	24	46	14	07	53	21	-01	20					
11. Teacher	12	18	02	12	-07	-04	15	30	43	03				
12. Landowner-Farmer	38	49	-12	20	00	04	36	19	22	15	17			
13. Small business person	23	24	16	09	07	-03	25	-18	-14	34	13	29		
14. Economic growth	-06	-07	59	22	14	46	-06	-26	-05	23	-30	-17	-06	
15. Per capita income	-15	-11	-50	-41	-07	-61	12	06	00	-27	21	-12	20	-36

Correlations above 28 are statistically significant at the 5 per cent level.

on rates of economic growth were calculated for the total set of 42 countries and, as in previous analyses, for the total set of 41 excluding the United Arab Emirates as an anomalous case, and for the subsets of 20 economically developed nations (those with GDPs of 3,000 US dollars and above, and excluding the United Arab Emirates) and the 21 economically developing nations. The results of the four multiple regressions are set out in *Table 27*. This gives the standardised regression coefficients for each of the variables on economic growth for the four sets of nations, ie the 'partial coefficients' or the coefficients for each variable holding all the other variables constant. The last two rows in the table give the multiple correlation and the square of the multiple correlation of the entire set of psychological variables with economic growth rates.

Table 27: Multiple regression analyses for psychological measures on rates of economic growth.

Psychological Measures	All Countries	41 Countries	Developed Countries	Developing Countries
Work Ethic	14	01	29	−08
Achievement Motivation	06	01	08	46
Mastery	−28	−16	−17	−26
Competitiveness	64	55	30	1.16
Achievement via Conformity	07	19	36	−08
Valuation of Money	11	21	71	−36
Attitudes to Saving	−11	00	−26	06
Doctor	−09	03	−22	12
Social Worker	12	11	−23	09
Company Director	−05	−17	24	−50
Teacher	−23	−31	08	−40
Country Landowner	21	−14	−44	29
Small Business Person	−17	−10	−16	−14
R (Multiple correlation)	63	71	63	87
R^2	40	50	40	76

The multiple regression analysis for the total set of countries shows that competitiveness is the only significant determinant of rates of economic growth. The other correlates of growth rates such as the valuation of money and of the occupation of company director have negligible effects when all other psychological measures are controlled. The partial regression coefficient of competitiveness on rates of economic growth of 0.64 is virtually identical with the multiple correlation of 0.63 for the entire set of psychological measures. The multiple correlation is squared to provide a measure of the percentage of the variance in economic growth rates which can be explained in terms of the psychological measures. The square of the multiple correlation is 0.40 and indicates that 40 per cent of the variation in economic growth rates can be attributed to national differences in the psychological measures, which are in effect confined to competitiveness. This also indicates that an increase in competitiveness of one standard deviation in a country could be expected to increase the rate of economic growth by 40 per cent of a standard deviation.

These inferences assume that the partial regression coefficient of 0.64 of competitiveness on economic growth rates is due to a one-way causal effect of the competitiveness of the population on rates of economic growth. It may be arguable that the causal sequence is in the other direction, ie that high rates of economic growth generate a high level of competitiveness in the population. It is not easy to see any reason why this should be the case, whereas it does seem plausible that a high level of competitiveness in a population could generate high economic growth rates because, as Schumpeter argued, if people have high competitiveness drives they are likely to work hard and productively and this will have a positive effect on economic growth. It is therefore proposed that the most reasonable interpretation of the multiple regression is that the level of competitiveness in the population makes a fairly substantial causal contribution amounting to 40 per cent of the variance in rates of economic growth.

When the United Arab Emirates are excluded the multiple regression is closely similar. Once again competitiveness is by far the most important contributor to economic growth rates. There are however a number of small additional contributions which make little contribution individually but together raise the multiple correlation to 0.71 and raise to 50 per cent the variance in rates of economic growth explained by the entire set of psychological measures.

The multiple regression analyses for the two subsets of the economically developed and the economically developing countries are also given in *Table 27*. Among the economically developed countries the valuation of money comes out as the most important determinant of economic growth rates. Addtional contributions to economic growth rates are made by the strength of the work ethic, competitiveness, achievement via conformity, valuation of the occupation of company director and negative valuation of the occupation of country landowner. The multiple correlation of all the psychological measures with economic growth rates is $+0.63$ and the square of the multiple correlation is 0.40, indicating that 40 per cent of the variance in economic growth rates can be explained in terms of the combined effects of this set of psychological measures in this set of countries.

The regression coefficients for the economically developing nations are shown in the fourth column of *Table 27*. As in the analysis for the total set of nations, competitiveness emerges as the most important determinant of economic growth rates. Achievement motivation also makes a contribution, while valuation of the occupation of company director apparently makes a negative contribution which is not easily explained. The multiple correlation of all the psychological measures with economic growth among the economically developing nations is $+87$ and the square of this correlation is 0.76, indicating that 76 per cent of the variance in economic growth rates can be explained in terms of the psychological measures among this set of countries.

The upshot of the multiple regression analyses is that among the total set of nations competitiveness is the only psychological factor contributing to rates of economic growth. Among the two subsets of the economically developed and economically developing nations the picture is more complex. Among the economically developed nations several psychological factors appear to exert independent effects, namely the valuation of money, work ethic, competitiveness, achievement via conformity, valuation of the occupation of company director and negative valuation of the occupation of country landowner and farmer. Among the economically developing nations competitiveness is again the major predictor of economic growth rates with some additional effect of achievement motivation. The results as a whole support Schumpeter's thesis of competitiveness as the major psychological variable affecting rates of economic growth. In addition, some support is present for Wiener's thesis that the relative valuations attached to the occupation of company director as compared with that attached to country landowner contributes to economic growth among the economically developed nations, while achievement motivation makes a contribution to economic growth among the economically developing countries.

13 Factor Analysis of Work Attitudes Across Countries

While the psychological measures used in the study provide measures of theoretically distinct constructs, it has been noted that several of them are quite highly correlated across countries. Where a number of measures are used and are intercorrelated it is possible to simplify them by factor analysis, which reduces the measures to a small number of underlying factors. These factors represent the common elements present in several measures.

There are several different methods of factor analysis but that most commonly employed is principal components analysis followed by varimax rotation. Principal components analysis normally produces a major general factor with which most or sometimes all of the variables are correlated or 'loaded' and also gives the number of significant factors in the correlation matrix. The method of varimax rotation gives a set of independent factors and the loadings (correlations) of the variables with these factors. The psychological meaning or nature of the factors can be identified from the variables with high loadings on them.

These analyses were carried out on the total sample of 41 countries (the United Arab Emirates and Transkei omitted) and the results are shown in *Table 28*. Four factors were found to be present (ie had eigenvalues above 1.0). The first factor can be identified as a broad work commitment factor which combines the work ethic, mastery and achievement via conformity scales. It may seem something of a curiosity that the occupation of country landowner and farmer should have the high loading of 0.51 on the factor. Probably the explanation for this is that the occupation of country landowner and farmer is widely regarded as yielding intrinsic satisfactions rather than large financial rewards, and therefore a high valuation for this occupation is associated with the broad work commitment factor. The second factor appears to be a broad competitiveness factor which combines competitiveness, saving and valuation of money. The third factor consists of favourable attitudes towards the caring professions with high loadings on the occupations of doctor, social worker and teacher and can be identified as a 'caring professions' factor. The fourth factor appears to be a positive attitude to business occupations with high loadings on the occupations of company director and small business owner. The small business owner has the highest loading, indicating that a favourable attitude towards this occupation taps some psychological motive which is not present among the traits measured in the study. Possibly this might be the need for independence from the power of others which has been identified by Collins, Moore and Unwalla as the primary motive which drives people into entrepreneurship.[47]

Table 28: Varimax analysis of work attitudes across countries

	Factor 1	Factor 2	Factor 3	Factor 4
Work ethic	89	02	07	–01
Mastery	82	15	13	06
Competitiveness	–03	82	–10	17
Savings	43	64	05	–25
Achievement Motivation	42	31	–42	–26
Valuation of Money	–00	92	02	08
Achievement via Conformity	75	–09	–00	24
Doctor	05	–21	80	01
Social worker	–00	26	80	–03
Company director	–01	57	14	62
Teacher	19	00	61	–06
Landowner-farmer	51	–00	40	13
Small business person	25	04	–10	75

The statistics of factor analysis require that there should be a reasonably small number of measures in relation to the number of 'subjects' (countries, in the present case) from which the measures are taken. For this reason it would not be valid to carry out factor analyses on the subsets of economically developed and economically developing countries because the numbers would be too small.

In addition to the advantage of simplifying the number of measures, factor analysis makes it possible to calculate the factor scores obtained by the countries on the factors. We can therefore calculate the score of each country on the first factor of work commitment and then calculate the correlation of these scores with rates of economic growth and per capita income. The same calculations can be made for the remaining factors. The factor scores are calculated by weighting each country's score on the psychological measures with the loading of these measures on the factors.

The correlations between the nations' factor scores on the four factors and rates of economic growth are shown in *Table 29* for the total sample of 41 nations and for the 20 economically developed and 21 economically developing nations. For the total sample of nations the broad competitiveness factor is correlated with economic growth at a statistically significant level of +0.52. This confirms the high correlation between the narrower competitiveness trait and economic growth and the emergence of competitiveness as the major psychological factor related to economic growth in the multiple regression analysis. The association between competitiveness and rates of economic growth holds among both the economically developed and the economically developing nations.

There is a significant tendency for the valuation of the caring professions to be negatively associated, correlated at −0.49, with economic growth among the economically developing nations, indicating that the more highly young people regard occupations like doctor, social worker and teacher, the poorer the national economic growth rates. There are no substantial or significant correlations between economic growth rates and either work commitment or the valuation of business occupations.

Table 29: Correlations between nations' factor scores on psychological measures and rates of economic growth (decimal points omitted)

Factors	All Countries	Developed Countries	Developing Countries
Work Commitment	−16	−09	−29
Competitiveness	52**	59**	39*
Caring Professions	−22	10	−49**
Business Occupations	−04	08	−07

Asterisks (1 and 2) denote statistical significance at the 5 and 1 per cent levels, respectively.

The correlations between the nations' factor scores on the four broad factors and national per capita income are shown in *Table 30* for the total sample, and for the developed and developing

93

countries separately. Competitiveness is associated in a negative
direction with per capita income in all three samples, and valuation
of the caring professions is positively associated with per capita income among the developed countries, suggesting that as people become more affluent they come to attach more value to the caring
professions.

*Table 30: Correlations between nations' factor scores on psychological
measures and per capita incomes*

Factors	All Countries	Developed Countries	Developing Countries
Work Commitment	−06	18	38*
Competitiveness	−55**	−38*	−34
Caring Professions	−01	38*	−24
Business Occupations	14	02	−11

Asterisks (1 and 2) denote statistical significance at the 5 and 1 per cent levels, respectively.

14 Factor Analyses of Work Attitudes within Countries

In this chapter we consider whether the four factors obtained from the factor analysis of the work attitudes measured across countries, presented in the last chapter, can also be obtained within countries. It has been stressed by Irvine and Berry that to make valid comparisons on psychological tests between populations in different countries it is desirable to show that the tests have the same factor structure in the respective countries.[48] In the present study it is not possible to present factor analyses for all the countries because most collaborators in the project sent in means and standard deviations for the measures rather than the raw data which are required for factor analysis. Nevertheless, there are several countries for which factor analyses are possible and these are presented. It will be noted that in the factor analysis presented in the last chapter the national means on the work attitude scales were factored and hence the nations were the 'subjects'. In this chapter the subjects are the individuals in several countries. It will be interesting to see whether the two methods produce the same factor structures.

In all the countries for which results are given in this chapter there were four significant factors and the varimax solution is shown. The results for the United States are given in *Table 31*. The four factors are very similar to the cross national analysis presented in the last chapter which produced the factors of work commitment, competitiveness, high valuation of the caring professions of doctor, social worker and teacher, and high valuation of the business occupations of company director and small business person. In the American data the first factor is work commitment, on which the four highest loadings are the work ethic, mastery, achievement motivation and achievement via conformity. The only difference from the across country analysis is that the occupation of country landowner and farmer has gone off this factor. The second factor is broad competitiveness on which the highest loadings are competitiveness and high valuation of money. There is also a fairly high loading for the occupation of company director, as in the cross national results. The third factor is the caring professions with high loadings for the occupations of doctor, social worker and teacher. The fourth factor is the business occupations with the highest loading of small business person and a high loading for company director, which splits about equally between the business occupations and competitiveness factors. Also well loaded on this factor is the occupation of country landowner and farmer. The reason for this is probably that this occupation is widely regarded as a form of small business in the United States and does not have the associations with an aristocrat's lifestyle on large country estates that tend to be present in Europe.

Table 31: Varimax analysis of work attitudes in the United States

	Factor 1	Factor 2	Factor 3	Factor 4
Work ethic	73	–03	08	03
Mastery	67	27	08	01
Competitiveness	11	73	–02	–05
Savings	44	00	–05	53
Achievement Motivation	82	05	00	04
Valuation of Money	–20	73	–12	21
Achievement via Conformity	66	–26	07	11
Doctor	04	39	58	09
Social worker	11	–06	69	–17
Company director	14	51	–09	47
Teacher	08	–30	70	–06
Landowner-farmer	–07	–14	49	58
Small business person	02	19	–17	68

The results for the United Kingdom are shown in *Table 32*. The first factor is work commitment with high loadings for work ethic, mastery, achievement motivation and achievement via conformity. The second factor is broad competitiveness with high loadings for competitiveness, valuation of money and the occupations of doctor and company director. The third factor is the caring professions with high loadings for the occupations of doctor, social worker and teacher. The fourth factor is business occupations with high loadings for country landowner and farmer and small business person. The factor structure is closely similar to that in the United States.

Table 32: Varimax analysis of work attitudes in the United Kingdom

	Factor 1	Factor 2	Factor 3	Factor 4
Work ethic	77	–09	00	–09
Mastery	73	08	04	–12
Competitiveness	33	64	–12	06
Savings	47	18	06	24
Achievement Motivation	76	30	–12	03
Valuation of Money	–09	75	–08	20
Achievement via Conformity	74	–00	03	11
Doctor	06	53	56	–13
Social worker	00	–08	76	–08
Company director	24	51	–24	44
Teacher	02	–18	73	13
Landowner-farmer	–14	12	21	64
Small business person	12	07	–18	78

The next country we consider is Australia. The four factors are shown in *Table 33*. The first factor is work commitment with high loadings for work ethic, mastery, achievement motivation and achievement via conformity. The second factor is broad competitiveness, with the high loadings of valuation of money and the occupation of company director. The competitiveness scale is a little lower on this factor than in the United States and the UK but is clearly present. The occupation of small business person has moved on to this factor in Australia. The third factor is the caring professions with the high loadings of social worker and teacher. Competitiveness has a high negative loading on this factor. The fourth factor is country landowner and farmer, probably reflecting the importance of these occupations in Australia.

Table 33: Varimax analysis of work attitudes in Australia

	Factor 1	Factor 2	Factor 3	Factor 4
Work ethic	71	–09	06	19
Mastery	70	01	–08	34
Competitiveness	31	34	–55	–00
Savings	23	63	33	–21
Achievement Motivation	77	27	–02	–16
Valuation of Money	–05	72	–33	08
Achievement via Conformity	66	15	14	–24
Doctor	30	19	–15	36
Social worker	08	–13	63	05
Company director	27	59	–38	02
Teacher	08	04	74	04
Landowner-farmer	–03	08	21	82
Small business person	01	64	–03	23

The results for New Zealand are shown in *Table 34*. The first factor is work commitment, with high loadings for work ethic, mastery, achievement motivation, and achievement via conformity. The second factor is broad competitiveness, with high loadings for competitiveness, valuation of money and the occupation of company director. The occupation of doctor also has a high loading on this factor in the New Zealand results. The third factor is the caring professions, with high loadings for the occupations of doctor, social worker and teacher. The fourth factor is business occupations, with high loadings for small business owner and company director.

Table 34: Varimax analysis of work attitudes in New Zealand

	Factor 1	Factor 2	Factor 3	Factor 4
Work ethic	66	–22	–02	17
Mastery	76	16	–02	–14
Competitiveness	20	67	–14	–07
Savings	39	19	–01	45
Achievement Motivation	73	30	–04	03
Valuation of Money	–14	61	–22	28
Achievement via Conformity	61	–02	05	29
Doctor	00	53	54	–15
Social worker	03	–13	71	–06
Company director	14	58	–00	42
Teacher	05	–10	73	00
Landowner-farmer	–18	–04	38	21
Small business person	08	05	02	83

We look now at the results for Singapore, a virtually totally urbanised city state and apparently a very different kind of society from the United States, the United Kingdom and Australia. The four factors are shown in *Table 35*.

The first factor is clearly work commitment (high loadings for work ethic, mastery, achievement motivation and achievement-via-conformity). The second factor is broad competitiveness (high loadings for competitiveness, valuation of money and the occupation of company director). The occupation of small business owner has moved on to this factor in Singapore, as in Australia. The third factor is the caring professions with the usual high loadings of social worker and teacher together with a curiously high loading for country landowner. The fourth factor is not the usual factor of business occupations but consists solely of the occupation of doctor. Both the business occupations of company director and small business

Table 35: Varimax analysis of work attitudes in Singapore

	Factor 1	Factor 2	Factor 3	Factor 4
Work ethic	68	04	09	−02
Mastery	68	15	−05	25
Competitiveness	27	46	−40	11
Savings	46	08	02	−23
Achievement Motivation	77	19	−20	11
Valuation of Money	−06	74	−11	−01
Achievement via Conformity	70	−25	07	−01
Doctor	13	−00	17	82
Social worker	17	−16	73	13
Company director	16	72	05	21
Teacher	12	−18	38	−57
Landowner-farmer	−14	23	68	−12
Small business person	08	62	22	−43

person have moved on to the competitiveness factor in Singapore suggesting that in this culture highly competitive persons direct their ambitions not only into the occupation of company director, as they do typically in other countries, but also into the occupation of small business person.

Another highly urbanised Pacific Rim economy, with a rather similar society to Singapore, is Hong Kong. The results of the factor analysis are shown in *Table 36*. The first factor is work commitment, with high loadings for work ethic, mastery, achievement motivation and achievement via conformity. The second factor is broad competitiveness with high loadings for competitiveness, valuation of money and the occupation of company director. The occupation of small business owner has moved on to this factor in Hong Kong, as in Australia and Singapore. The third factor is the caring professions, with high loadings for social worker and teacher. The fourth factor is a rather curious combination of the occupations of doctor and country landowner and farmer.

There can be few countries as far removed from the economically developed capitalist economies of the United States, the United Kingdom and Australia as the People's Republic of China, and it will therefore be interesting to see whether the factor structure of the measures of work attitudes among Chinese students bears any resemblance to that in the advanced economies of the West. The results are shown in *Table 37*. The first factor is the same work commitment factor as was obtained in the other nations, with high loadings for work ethic, mastery, achievement motivation

Table 36: Varimax analysis of work attitudes in Hong Kong

	Factor 1	Factor 2	Factor 3	Factor 4
Work ethic	63	23	23	–09
Mastery	73	09	03	13
Competitiveness	33	62	–04	–18
Savings	48	28	32	–12
Achievement Motivation	66	04	–13	–03
Valuation of Money	–08	71	–01	12
Achievement via Conformity	66	–30	–03	10
Doctor	–01	06	14	68
Social worker	11	–09	77	16
Company director	19	49	–09	34
Teacher	–05	07	78	06
Landowner-farmer	01	07	05	70
Small business person	–00	62	09	08

and achievement via conformity. The second factor is the same broad competitiveness factor as has been found elsewhere, combining competitiveness, valuation of money and the occupations of company director or 'head of large organisation' in the Chinese version of the questionnaire. The third factor is the caring professions of doctor, social worker and teacher, as found in other countries. The fourth factor consists of the two occupations of country landowner and farmer and small business person, again as found in the United States and Britain. Thus in the very different culture of China we find a very similar factor structure of work attitudes to that obtained in the developed economies of the West.

Table 37: Varimax analysis of work attitudes in China

	Factor 1	Factor 2	Factor 3	Factor 4
Work ethic	67	–17	15	–07
Mastery	73	12	01	–08
Competitiveness	56	45	–02	–20
Savings	02	36	42	08
Achievement Motivation	75	11	–03	07
Valuation of Money	–03	76	–00	18
Achievement via Conformity	48	–36	02	31
Doctor	–10	28	59	–28
Social worker	04	–05	68	17
Company director	37	54	–05	24
Teacher	12	–25	68	08
Landowner-farmer	–03	02	18	69
Small business person	–06	36	–05	72

Table 38: Varimax analysis of work attitudes in Japan

	Factor 1	Factor 2	Factor 3	Factor 4
Work ethic	61	03	02	02
Mastery	64	12	04	−08
Competitiveness	29	50	19	−11
Savings	30	−02	−22	36
Achievement Motivation	51	43	−08	−01
Valuation of Money	−09	16	22	25
Achievement via Conformity	57	−04	17	38
Doctor	−03	05	−01	38
Social worker	13	−21	09	29
Company director	−03	−23	66	28
Teacher	39	07	50	−04
Landowner-farmer	−02	56	−08	13
Small business person	−01	−06	−14	25

The final country for which the factor structure of the attitudes to work scales was examined was Japan. The data are based on 238 students from Doshisha University and the results are shown in *Table 38*. The first factor is the familiar work commitment with high loadings for work ethic, mastery, achievement motivation and achievement via conformity. The second factor is broad competitiveness, with high loadings for competitiveness and valuation of money. The third factor is landowner-farmer and small business person and should probably be regarded as a factor of small business owner. The fourth factor is the caring professions factor with high loadings for the occupations of social worker, teacher and doctor. In addition, the occupation of company director has moved on to this factor in Japan, perhaps reflecting a stronger dimension of social commitment in the management of large companies in Japan as compared with the West.

The conclusions from these factorial studies are that the factor structure of work attitudes across countries and within the eight sample countries is closely similar, even among such dissimilar societies as the advanced capitalist economies of the United States, Britain, Australia and New Zealand, the capitalist city states of Singapore and Hong Kong, the communist society of the Peoples' Republic of China and the dynamic economy of Japan. All the analyses produce essentially the same four factors of work commitment, competitiveness, the valuation of the caring professions and the valuation of the business occupations. There are some small differences of detail, as where the occupation of small business person is associated with the broad competitiveness factor in Singapore, whereas in the other countries and in the across nation analysis it appears as the core of the fourth factor. Nevertheless, the overall picture is clearly one of a high degree of consistency in all the analyses, both across and within nations.

15 Epilogue

The single most important result of the study is that the level of competitiveness in a society has emerged as the psychological factor most significantly related to the rate of economic growth. The other three leading theories of psychological attitudes underlying economic growth – the work ethic, achievement motivation, and a low valuation of business – do not receive any confirmation from the study and can therefore be ruled out as significant determinants of differences in economic growth rates among contemporary nations. These other attitudes may well have made a contribution to economic growth rates at other historic periods but they do not appear to be operative today.

The substantial correlation between national levels of competitiveness and rates of economic growth does not of course establish causation. However, it is a phenomenon that requires explanation and it is incumbent on sceptics to offer some alternative theory for how the correlation arises. There are two other possibilities. One is that high rates of economic growth generate competitiveness in the population, but it is not at all clear why or how this could occur. The second alternative is that some common factor affects both the level of competitiveness and the rate of economic growth, but here again it is not easy to think of what such a factor might be. It is considered therefore that the result goes some way to providing an empirical test and confirmation of the thesis advanced more than 50 years ago by Schumpeter to the effect that the competitiveness of the people is the crucial psychological factor in explaining why growth rates differ between nations.

It is easy to understand how a highly competitive people would achieve a high rate of national economic growth. Competitive people expend effort to win status and for many people this means making money. It is therefore particularly interesting that our study should have found that highly competitive people attach a lot of importance to money. The valuation of money and competitiveness were found to be highly associated among individuals within countries and also across countries. This association between the competitiveness and the valuation of money provides one of the mechanisms through which a high level of national competitiveness generates a high rate of economic growth. Where there are a lot of competitive people, there are a lot of people who badly want to make money. The way to make money is to produce goods and services which other people are prepared to buy. It is the efficient production of goods and services that generates economic growth.

If the role of competitiveness in economic growth rates is granted, the question inevitably arises of whether it would be either desirable or possible to raise the level of competitiveness in the population as a means of increasing the rate of economic growth. There will be a variety of different opinions on this question according to how people fall along what the early psychologist, William James, called the 'tough-minded - tender-minded' dimension of human temperament.[49] The tough-minded are happy enough with economic growth and competition as part of a social order in which the strong succeed and the weak go to the wall, whereas the tender-minded recoil from a society where those who fail have to suffer the consequences.

In the contemporary world an influential expression of the tender-minded temperament is the Greens. These people are opposed to further economic growth. Their argument is that economic growth uses up the world's natural resources, causes widespread pollution, is responsible for the greenhouse effect and the depletion of the ozone layer, will create deserts in Africa, Asia and America, cause a rise in sea levels through global warming which will flood many low-lying areas, and generally bring about global catastrophe. On these grounds, the Greens argue that economic growth should cease and people should be encouraged to adopt a simple 'back to nature' lifestyle, growing their own fruit and vegetables, generating electricity by windmills, travelling by bicycle and doing everything possible to conserve natural resources. For the Greens the findings of our study indicate that the way to induce the changes of attitude necessary to bring about such a change in lifestyle lies in reducing the competitiveness of the population. If people could be made less competitive they would cease to desire many of the consumer goods which are responsible for the world's pollution.

But for many people the Green vision of the world is neither true nor desirable. The mainstream view among economists is that economic growth yields benefits in enhanced human happiness, choice, welfare and health. The solution to industrial pollution is more economic growth rather than less, because economic growth provides the money required to deal with the pollution. For instance, coal-fired electricity power stations produce sulphur dioxide which causes pollution, but it is possible – at a cost – to reduce these emissions. Similarly, the cheapest thing to do with industrial waste is generally to dump it in the nearest river. This pollutes the river and kills the fish and other wildlife and is undesirable. It is always possible to dispose of the industrial waste elsewhere, but at greater cost. All that is required to overcome pollution is money, and the money comes from economic growth.

If we decide that economic growth is desirable, the study suggests that economic growth rates could be increased by making people more competitive. There are many people who would not like this, not because they are Greens, but because their tender-mindedness takes a different form and they feel that there is something unhealthy or undesirable about the motive of competitiveness. Central to this view is the concern that where there is competition there have to be losers as well as winners. Competition is fine for people who are intelligent, healthy, socially advantaged and industrious and are therefore likely to be among the winners. But it is not so good for those who lack these advantages, are going to be the losers and are likely to become alienated from society.

Another component in the thinking of those who dislike competition is that there is something selfish or even immoral about the competitive drive. The highly competitive person simply wants to prove himself or herself (generally himself) better than others, to put them down, even humiliate them, and demonstrate that he or she (generally he) is smarter than others. What motive could be more petty, degraded or more unworthy of civilised people? Throughout history people have yearned for a better way, to build a society in which people are motivated to work in co-operation and in a spirit of brotherly love and the baser motives of self-advancement are banished. This has been the ideal of socialism. It may be that the experience of socialism in the Soviet Union, Eastern Europe and China suggests that the ideal does not work well in practice. But maybe this is just because in these countries the ideal was not correctly implemented and that, learning from these experiences, the socialist ideal of a co-operative rather than a competitive society could still be made to work.

Set against these views is the tough-minded tradition which regards competition as a positive good and the engine of progress in general as well as of economic growth. This tradition is rooted in both biology and in social science. In biology it is expressed in Charles Darwin's theory of evolution which states that it is through competition between individuals and species that evolutionary progress has taken place. Less efficient and capable individuals and species have been progressively eliminated and have become extinct, leaving increasingly efficient and capable individuals and species as the survivors. Without competition human beings would never have evolved. Human beings are the supremely successful competitors in the evolutionary struggle and have done so well that we have achieved mastery over the world and all other species, except for our greatest enemy, the bacteria who still remain to be conquered.

It is not only biology which identifies competition as the mechanism through which progress is achieved: the same theory holds in the social sciences. It was first set out systematically in 1776 by Adam Smith in *The Wealth of Nations*. Smith argued that every man working to further his own advantage, in competition with others doing similar work, is the process through which a society grows prosperous. Does the baker sell bread through motives of altruism to further the public good, Smith asked? Of course not. The baker sells bread to make money for himself and his family. And by doing this, and by being allowed to make money, the baker's selfish motives allow the public to buy cheap bread and promote public well-being. If the baker is not permitted to sell bread at a profit to himself, he will not sell bread at all. Anyone who doubts this should pay a visit to Moscow and see for themselves.

The best contemporary re-statement of Adam Smith's thesis is F A Hayek's *The Constitution of Liberty*. Today this is the leading theory in economics and political economy. Thus the biological theory derived from Darwin and the economic theory derived from Adam Smith both place competition as the mechanism through which progress is achieved at the centre of their theoretical edifices. In fact, economics can be regarded as a branch of the more general biological theory of evolution: the branch dealing with the application to human economic affairs of the principle of competition leading to progressive improvement through the survival of the fittest.

If it is granted that economic growth is desirable and that competition as a means of achieving economic growth is also desirable, the question needs to be considered, whether it would be possible to increase the competitiveness of young people as a means of enhancing economic growth. The psychological principles that would be employed to achieve this objective are reasonably clear. Values, attitudes and behaviour are developed by rewarding them or, in more technical psychological terminology, through the administration of positive reinforcements. Many parents use this principle to encourage competitiveness in their children, as when they give praise or presents when their children do well in school or in games. Many teachers also use this method when they award grades or marks for good work, and prizes or trophies for success in sports. Parents and teachers already have a broad but amateurish understanding of how competitiveness is developed.

To increase the level of competitiveness in young people would require a more systematic application of these psychological principles and a close examination of societies like those of the Pacific Rim to analyse how their high levels of competitiveness are achieved. The problem of how to deal with losers in the competitive process would also need to be addressed to mitigate the damaging effects of alienation and low self-esteem that inevitably accompany failure in competitive endeavour. The way to surmount this problem is through the application of the principle that *everyone can be good at something*. The principle is not strictly true, but it has enough truth to be useful for dealing with this problem. At present schools place great emphasis on verbal learning and ability and give little attention to the development of visuo-spatial abilities which are employed in engineering, design, building and the craft skills. Many adolescents who lack strong verbal ability do poorly in schools and become alienated, but they have strong visuo-spatial abilities which could be developed and which would allow them to succeed in fields where those with strong verbal abilities are unable to compete. There are still other areas where those with modest academic abilities can achieve success, such as music, art and sport. This is the way to overcome the problem of the alienation of losers to which critics of competition have rightly pointed.

I believe therefore that this study has identified the hitherto missing component in economists' accounts of why growth rates differ between nations. The missing ingredient is the competitiveness of the people. Adam Smith set out the basics of the theory more than two centuries ago and Schumpeter guessed it correctly in the 1930s. Now for the first time the theory has been put on a sound empirical basis.

Notes and References

1. Max Weber, *The Protestant Ethic and the Spirit of Capitalism*, 1904 (Translated by T Parsons, New York: Scribner 1929).
2. J Woronoff, *Asia's Miracle Economies*, New York: M E Sharpe, 1986.
3. D S Landes, 'Why are we so rich and they so poor?', *American Economic Review* 80, 1990, pp 1-13.
4. D C McClelland, *The Achieving Society*, Princeton: Van Nostrand, 1976.
5. Martin J Wiener, *English Culture and the Decline of the Industrial Spirit 1850-1980*, Cambridge University Press, 1981.
6. D Bell, *The Coming of the Post-Industrial Society*, London: Heinemann, 1974.
7. R Katzell and D Yankelovich, *Work, Productivity and Job Satisfaction*, New York: Psychological Corporation, 1976.
8. A Furnham, *The Protestant Work Ethic*, Oxford: Pergamon Press, 1990.
9. B Stafford, *The End of Economic Growth? Growth and Decline in the UK since 1945*, Oxford: Martin Robertson, 1981.
10. A Madison, 'The long run dynamics of productivity growth.' in W Beckerman (ed), *Slow Growth in Britain*, Oxford: Clarendon Press, 1979.
11. E F Denison, *Why Growth Rates Differ*, Washington DC: The Brookings Institution, 1967.
12. J Vaizey, *The Political Economy of Education*, London: Duckworth, 1972.
13. Weber, op cit.
14. H A L Fisher, *A History of Europe*, London: Arnold, 1936.
15. H Trevor-Roper, *Religion, The Reformation and other Essays*, London: Macmillan, 1967.
16. R H Tawney, *Religion and the Rise of Capitalism*, London: Murray, 1936.
17. H L Mirels and J B Garrett. 'The Protestant ethic as a personality variable', *Journal of Consulting and Clinical Psychology* 36, 1971, pp 40-44.
18. A Furnham,'The Protestant work ethic: a review of the psychological literature', *European Journal of Social Psychology* 14, 1984, pp 87-104.
19. J A Schumpeter, *The Theory of Economic Development*, Oxford University Press, 1934.
20. McClelland, op cit.
21. S U Ahmed 'N Ach, risk-taking propensity, locus of control and entrepreneurship', *Personality and Individual Differences* 6, 1985, pp 781-2.
22. O F Collins, D G Moore and D B Unwalla, *The Enterprising Man*, East Lansing: University of Michigan Press, 1964.
23. D C McClelland, *Motivating Economic Achievement*.
24. McClelland, *Achieving Society*, op cit.
25. L J Finison, "The application of McClelland's national development model to recent data', *Journal of Social Psychology* 98, 1986, pp 55-59.
26. Wiener, op cit.
27. McClelland, *Achieving Society*, op cit.

28. G Hofstede, *Culture's Consequences: International Differences in Work-Related Values*, London: Sage, 1980.
29. Weber, op cit.
30. J A Spence and R L Helmreich, 'Achievement related motives and behavior' in J T Spence (ed), *Achievment and Achievement Motives*, San Francisco: W H Freeman, 1983.
31. Ibid.
32. McClelland, *Achieving Society*, op cit.
33. A Furnham and A Lewis, *The Economic Mind*, Brighton, UK: Wheatsheaf, 1986
34. R Lynn, 'An achievement motivation questionnaire', *British Journal of Psychology* 60, 1969, pp 526-534.
35. J J Ray, 'A quick measure of achievement motivation – validated in Australia and reliable in Britain and South Africa', *Australian Psychologist* 14, 1979, pp 337-345.
36. M S Horner, 'Femininity and successful achievement: a basic inconsistency', in J M Barwick, E Donvan, M S Horner and D Guttman (eds), *Feminine Precedent and Conflict*, Belmont CA: Brooks-Cole, 1970.
37. K W Fischer and A Lazerson, *Human Development*, New York: W H Freeman, 1984.
38. Spence and Helmreich, op. cit.
39. Schumpeter, op cit.
40. Spence and Helmreich, op cit.
41. J Lopreato, *Human Nature and Biocultural Evolution*, Boston: Allen and Unwin, 1984.
42. W H Whyte, *The Organisation Man*, Garden City: Doubleday, 1956.
43. See for example F J Landy and D A Trumbo, *Psychology of Work Behavior*, Homewood: Dorsey, 1980.
44. A Furnham, 'Many sides of the coin: the psychology of money usage', *Personality and Individual Differences* 5, 1984, pp 501-9.
45. K T Yamauchi and D I Templer, 'The development of a money attitude scale', *Journal of Personality Assessment* 46, 1982, pp 522-8.
46. Wiener, op cit.
47. Collins, Moore and Unwalla, op cit.
48. S H Irvine and J W Berry, 'The abilities of mankind: a revaluation', in S H Irvine and J W Berry (eds), *Human Abilities in Cultural Context*, Cambridge University Press, 1988.
49. W James, *Principles of Psychology*, London: Macmillan, 1890.

Biographical Note

Richard Lynn is Professor of Psychology at the University of Ulster. He has been Lecturer in Psychology at the University of Exeter; Research Fellow at the Neuro-Psychiatric Institute, Princeton; and Professor of Psychology at the Dublin Economic and Social Research Institute. He is author of *Arousal, Attention and the Orientation Reaction; The Universities and the Business Community; The Irish Brain Drain; Personality and National Character; Introduction to the Study of Personality;* and *Educational Achievement in Japan: Lessons for the West;* and editor of *The Entrepreneur* and *Dimensions of Personality.*

The Social Affairs Unit

The Unit is a research and educational trust committed to the promotion of lively and wide-ranging debate on social affairs. Its authors – now numbering over 100 – have analysed the factors which make for a free and orderly society in which enterprise can flourish. Their studies have included the reform of social security, the relation of education to business and enterprise, school standards, police accountability, housing, criminal deterrence, the media, the environment, family matters and the churches and social issues.

An increasingly significant extension to the Unit's work is introducing the press and broadcast media to authors and speakers and providing background research on a wide range of social issues. Unit authors have been asked to write for *The Times, The Daily Telegraph, The Daily Mail, The Sunday Telegraph, The Spectator, The Times Education* and *Higher Education Supplements, The Wall Street Journal, The National Review* (USA) as well as many specialist journals. Television appearances have included *Panorama, Newsweek, Heart of the Matter, Thinking Aloud, The Jimmy Young Show* and many others. The Unit has also provided speakers for national and local radio programmes, the BBC World Service and academic conferences. All this is in addition to visits to speak at schools and universities.

Some responses to the Unit's work

'An intellectual counter-attack is under way from the Social Affairs Unit'

The Guardian

'The Social Affairs Unit [has] played a key role in testing...ideas on public opinion over the last ten years... Its influence is behind the Prime Minister's recent emphasis on... values'

The Independent

'The Social Affairs Unit has done a service for the country by bringing these facts [on nutrition policy] to our attention'

Hansard

'Almost alone among the think tanks [in] questioning the status quo on law and order has been the Social Affairs Unit'

The Spectator

'A Social Affairs Unit [publication] would not merit the name unless it were provocative'

New Society

'The Social Affairs Unit is famous for driving its coach and horses through the liberal consensus, scattering intellectual picket lines as it goes. It is equally famous for raising questions which strike most people most of the time as too dangerous or too difficult to think about'

The Times

SOME PUBLICATIONS FROM THE SOCIAL AFFAIRS UNIT

On Education

Educational Achievement in Japan: Lessons for The West
Richard Lynn
'... finds that teacher motivation in Japan is fuelled by two factors: having to teach to a national curriculum and working in schools which have to compete on results to survive.'   *Times Educational Supplement*
Studies in Social Revaluation 1
Published in co-operation with The Macmillan Press
Casebound: ISBN 0 333 44531 7 £29.50
Paperback: ISBN 0 333 44532 5 £8.95

The Wayward Curriculum: A Cause for Parents' Concern?
Edited by Dennis O'Keeffe
'This excellent collection'   *Times Higher Educational Supplement*
ISBN 0 907631 19 3 £9.95 casebound

Trespassing? Businessmen's Views On The Education System
Michael Brophy et al
'... much of what the industrialists say would be readily embraced by people in the LEAs and activists in the teaching profession'   *Education*
ISBN 0 907631 11 8 £2.95

Educated for Employment?
Digby Anderson et al
'...the [SAU] has turned its attention to the need for a more precisely governed relationship between educator and employer'
Times Higher Education Supplement
ISBN 0 907631 03 7 £2.65

The Pied Pipers of Education
Antony Flew et al
'The SAU has chosen a provocative role in an attempt to improve real debate about the ground rules for education and welfare'
Times Higher Education Supplement
0 907631 02 9 £2.65

Schooling for British Muslims: Integrated, Opted-out or Denominational?
Mervyn Hiskett
'A reasoned case in favour of creating separate state-funded Muslim schools'
The Times
Research Report 12
ISBN 0 907631 33 9 £4.50

Who Teaches the Teachers? A Contribution to Public Debate of the DES Green Paper
Anthony O'Hear
'makes out a powerful case for opening up our schools to motivated, qualified would-be teachers who have not been through the mill of departments of education'
Daily Telegraph
Research Report 10
ISBN 0 907631 31 2 £3.00

Detecting Bad Schools: A Guide for Normal Parents
Digby Anderson
'combines sense with humour...never dull..if it alerts parents to their rights... and reminds teachers of their responsibilities to parents, it can do a lot of good'
The Universe

ISBN 0 907631 04 5 £1.00

On law and order...

Deterring Potential Criminals
Ernest van den Haag
'will most probably have a considerable influence'
Howard Journal of Criminal Justice

Research Report 7
ISBN 0 907631 14 2 £2.00

Are The Police Fair? A New Light On the Sociological Evidence
P A J Waddington
'Sociologists rapped for anti-police bias'
Police Review
Research Report 2
ISBN 0 907631 07 X £1.00

Are The Police Under Control?
David Regan
'a good case'   *Daily Telegraph*
Research Report 1
ISBN 0 907631 06 1 £1.00

Criminal Welfare On Trial *Colin Brewer et al*
'Its new and astringent mix of pragmatism and genuine social concern... is bound
to attract a positive response'   *Church Times*
ISBN 0 907631 01 1 £2.65

On the welfare state...

**Popular Attitudes to State Welfare Provision: A Growing Demand for
Alternatives?**
Peter Saunders and Colin Harris
'suggest[s] that the public feels "trapped" into supporting state services by
taxation because people are unable or unwilling to pay twice'   *Sunday Times*
Research Report 11
ISBN 0 907631 30 4 £3.00

Action On Welfare: Reform of Personal Income Taxation and Social Security
Hermione Parker
'...represent[s] an important contribution to the debate on social policy the
Government cannot ignore'   *The Times*
Research Report 4
ISBN 0 907631 04 5 £2.00

From Cradle To Grave: Comparative Perspectives on the State of Welfare
Ralph Segalman and David Marsland
Studies in Social Revaluation 2
Published in co-operation with The Macmillan Press
Casebound ISBN 0 333 47004 4 £29.50
Paperback ISBN 0 333 47005 2 £8.95

Breaking The Spell Of The Welfare State
Digby Anderson, June Lait & David Marsland
'almost as critical of the present government's strategies as the policies of previous
Labour administrations'   *The Guardian*
ISBN 0 907631 00 2 £2.65

on family matters...

Full Circle? Bringing up Children in the Post-Permissive Society
Edited by Digby Anderson
'A timely new study... makes a powerful plea for a return to bringing up our
children in traditional ways'   *Daily Mail*
ISBN 0 907631 29 0 £8.95

Denying Homes to Black Children: Britain's New Race Adoption Policies
David Dale
'challenges the view that transracial adoption can be psychologically harmful'
                                                                       The Scotsman
Research Report 8
ISBN 0 907631 32 1 £3.50

Finding Fault in Divorce
George Brown
'... good advice. Our guess is that the Prime Minister will take it to heart.'
                                                                       Daily Mail
Moral Aspects of Social Problems 1
ISBN 0 907631 32 0 £3.50

On health...

A Diet Of Reason: Sense and Nonsense in the Healthy Eating Debate
Edited by Digby Anderson
'.. a complex, sensible and badly needed book'   *New Scientist*
ISBN 0 907631 26 6 £9.95 casebound
ISBN 0 907631 22 3 £5.95 paperback

Drinking to Your Health: The Allegations and the Evidence
Edited by Digby Anderson
'..based on the conclusions of academics and doctors... a major challenge to the
thinking on alcohol abuse.'   *Daily Mail*
ISBN 0907 631 37 1 £14.95 casebound
ISBN 0907 631 38 X £9.95 paperback

On the environment and housing...

After Government Failure?
D.R. Denman
Taking Thought for the Environment 1
ISBN 0 907631 24 X £2.50
Planning Fails The Inner Cities
R.N. Goodchild and D.R. Denman
Taking Thought for the Environment 2
ISBN 0 907631 25 8 £2.50
Caring for the Countryside: Public Dependence on Private Interest
Barry Bracewell-Milnes
Taking Thought for the Environment 3
ISBN 0 907631 27 4 £2.50
'refute the widespread contention that the greatest harm done to the environment is by individuals [and] cite a number of initiatives taken by companies and individuals to safeguard and improve the environment in which they live and work'
Financial Times

Home Truths
Barbara Robson et al
'illustrate[s] the need for members to be aware of the chasm that too often yawns between even progressive housing policies and how they work out in practice'
Local Government Chronicle
ISBN 0 907631 05 3 £2.95

Asian Housing In Britain
Jon Davies
'...a broadside attack on academic research into immigrant housing'
New Society
Research Report 6
ISBN 0 907631 13 4 £2.00

On moral and social issues

The Kindness That Kills: The Church's Simplistic Response To Complex Social Issues
Edited by Digby Anderson
'an excellent point of reference... sets out succinctly the feebleness, predictability, ignorance and uncharitableness of so many church productions'
Charles Moore, *The Spectator*
Commissioned by the SAU and published by SPCK
ISBN 0 281 04096 6 £3.95

Wealth And Poverty: A Jewish Analysis
Jonathan Sacks
Taking Thought for the Poor 1
ISBN 0 907631 15 0 £2.00
The Bible, Justice And The Culture Of Poverty: Emotive Calls to Action Versus Rational Analysis
Irving Hexham
Taking thought for the Poor 2
ISBN 0 907631 16 9 £2.00
The Philosophy Of Poverty: Good Samaritans or Procrusteans
Antony Flew
Taking Thought for the Poor 3
ISBN 0 907631 17 7 £2.00
The Christian Response To Poverty: Working with God's Economic Laws
James Sadowsky
Taking thought for the Poor 4
ISBN 0 907631 18 5 £2.00
'The most devastating criticism of the views which the Christian Churches in the West now regularly proclaim on this matter' T.E. Utley, *The Daily Telegraph*

Why Social Policy Cannot be Morally Neutral: The Current Confusion about Pluralism
Basil Mitchell
Moral Aspects of Social Problems 2
ISBN 0 907631 35 5 £3.50

Self-Improvement and Social Action
Antony Flew
Moral Aspects of Social Problems 3
'Those with influence, including the Churches, should... insist on the individual responsibility which comes with free choice.'
Daily Telegraph
ISBN 0 907631 36 3 £3.50

Consumer Debt: Whose Responsibility?
K Alec Chrystal
Moral Aspects of Social Problems 4
ISBN 0 907631 39 8 £3.50

Do Animal Have Rights?
Tibor Machan
Morals Aspects of Social Problems 5
ISBN 0 907631 40 1 £3.50,

On the media...

The Megaphone Solution: Government Attempts to Cure Social Problems with Mass Media Campaigns
Digby Anderson
'will undoubtedly cause a furore'   *Marketing*
Research Report 9
ISBN 0 907631 28 2 £3.00

Tracts Beyond The Times: A Brief Guide to the Communist or Revolutionary Marxist Press
Charles Ellwell
'I can warmly recommend it... a valuable guide'

Bernard Levin, *The Times*

Research Report 3
ISBN 0 907631 08 8 £1.50

on affirmative action...

Reversing Racism: Lessons from America
Kenneth M Holland & Geoffrey Parkins
'Britain... warned today against emulating the American pattern of positive discrimination'   *The Times*
Research Report 5
ISBN 0 907631 10 X £2.00

And...

Set Fair: A Gradualist Proposal for Privatising Weather Forecasting
Jerome Ellig
'Here is a ripe case for privatisation with competition built in as part of the package...'   *Today*
Research Report 13
ISBN 0 907631 34 7 £4.50

Extra Dry: Columns in The Times
Digby Anderson
'imperative writing on political and social subjects.'   *The Spectator*
ISBN 0 907631 12 6 £2.95